Flickering
Bible
Characters 1

Study Guide

Noel and Denise Enete

Spectrum Bible

Published by Spectrum Bible™, *spectrumbible.com*
Available from Amazon, *amazon.com*
Edition 1.0.0

Scripture quotations noted **NIV** are taken from the HOLY BIBLE, NEW INTERNATIONAL VERSION. Copyright 1973, 1978, and 1984 by International Bible Society. Used by permission of Zondervan Publishing House. All rights reserved.

Scripture quotations noted **NASB** are taken from the NEW AMERICAN STANDARD BIBLE, Copyright 1960, 1962, 1963, 1968, 1971, 1972, 1973, 1975, 1977, by The Lockman Foundation. Used by permission.

The FLCR study strategy was adapted from Robert A. Traina's Methodical Bible Study, Copyright 1952 by Robert A. Traina and Anne Graham Lotz's Living a Life that is Blessed, Copyright 1995 by AnGel Ministries.

ISBN 978-0-9791595-8-9

Printed and bound in the United States of America

Table Of Contents

"God
   has made promises
   that He will keep
   because He is good,
   not because
   we are good."

the Authors

Preface

One of the things God did to comfort and reassure us when He wrote His word was to include the good and bad traits of His heroes of the faith. It would have been very easy to leave out their flaws. It would certainly have been less embarrassing for Him.

But He presented realistic and approachable characters and how they worshiped and served Him. These are both people we can relate to and people we can be inspired by. Faith and good behavior that grows out of a context of need demonstrates that God's people of all ages are real and their behavior is within our reach.

As you *Flicker* their lives notice how God reacts to their strengths and how He reacts to their weaknesses. Notice what pleases Him and what He is just putting up with.

Also notice the difficulties these people struggle with and the ways they soar in their faith and devotion. How does Sarah handle having to wait for such a long time? How does Rahab handle the need to disobey the authorities? How does Abigail handle being married to a fool? How does Ruth make impossible choices?

God has much to teach us through these lives.

Organization Of The Book

The format of this book encourages you to write out what you notice in the passages and respond to God accordingly. Then as you explore these passages, also be alert to notice what you can learn about what God is like.

If you are not familiar with *Flicker Bible Study,* an explanation and example follows.

How To Flicker The Bible

Facts

In the *Facts* panel, make a list of the *Facts* you see in the passage. You don't have to list all the details. Just try and find the main points. You can use the same words as are in the passage. You will usually get somewhere around four to six *Facts*.

Lessons

In the *Lessons* panel, look over the list of facts and see what you can learn from the passage. Look for what seems unusual in the passage and often you'll find a *Lesson* there. Also, consider what you can learn about God from this passage? What does He value? What does He respond to? What pleases Him? You don't have to find a *Lesson* from every verse. Usually you will get one or two *Lessons* from a whole passage.

Challenges

In the *Challenges* panel, turn each *Lesson* you identified into a question that *Challenges* you. Listen for God to speak to you. He may not speak to you through every verse, but He will speak to you. You will normally get the same number of *Challenges* as *Lessons*.

Response

In the *Response* panel, consider what God is saying to you through this passage and decide how you will respond. Write out your *Response* as a two or three sentence prayer.

Be heartfelt and honest with God. If needed, put "training wheels" on your *Response*: "Lord help me to want this." Better to be honest and ask for help, than promise behavior you are not ready to keep.

History Of Flicker Bible Study

We have taught *Flicker Bible Study* in person and over the Internet to thousands of people in person since starting in 2004. But where did this Bible study method come from?

Flicker Bible Study came from the *Inductive Bible Study* method. During the post World War II rise in self-help books, Robert Traina (then Dean of Asbury Theological Seminary) wrote the first book that described a "method" of studying the Bible. The book was called **Methodical Bible Study** and the method became known as the *Inductive Bible Study* method. Before that point, Bible study was considered part of the hermeneutics discipline of a theological curriculum. Traina simplified the steps and coined the terms *Observation, Interpretation, Application,* and a few others. He taught a skill-based course out of Asbury that generated a lot of excitement around the idea that everyone could understand the Bible. Howard Hendricks (then Professor at Dallas Theological Seminary) attended Traina's course and created a similar course at Dallas Theological Seminary that equipped a generation of Bible teachers (including the present authors) to help people study the Bible using the *Inductive Bible Study* method.

Ann Graham Lotz (daughter of Billy Graham) uses a 4-step variation of the *Inductive Bible Study* method. In her writings the *Observation* step is called "List the Facts," the *Interpretation* step is "Learn from the Lessons," and the *Application* step is split into a pivotal step called "Listen to His Voice" and a response step called "Live in Response." The present authors have found that splitting the *Application* step into this kind of pivotal question and response is an improvement that helps more people grasp how a passage touches their life.

Flicker Bible Study modifies the names of the steps of *Inductive Bible Study* so that they are less abstract, easier to grasp, and easier to remember: *Observation* becomes *(F)acts,Interpretation* becomes *(L)essons,* the pivotal step "Listen to His Voice" becomes *(C)hallenges,* and *Application* becomes *(R)esponses.*

So, Robert Traina (father of *Inductive Bible Study*) taught the method to Howard Hendricks (Professor Dallas Theological Seminary) who taught it to the present authors who added the pivotal step from Ann Graham Lotz and simplified the names of the steps to spell *FLCR* which is pronounced *Flicker.*

Example—Psalm 121

To get an idea how to *Flicker* a Bible passage, the following pages present *Psalm 121* with the *Flicker* steps filled in. This is a guide to help you understand what kind of item goes in each panel.

More items are included in these panels than you would normally write in your study of a passage. More are included to give you more examples so you have a better idea what goes in each panel.

For more explanation of *Flicker Bible Study* see our book, *Flicker Bible Study* available from *amazon.com.*

Example—Psalm 121

Psalms 121:1 I lift up my eyes to the mountains; From where shall my help come?

Psalms 121:2 My help [comes] from the LORD, Who made heaven and earth.

Psalms 121:3 He will not allow your foot to slip; He who keeps you will not slumber.

Psalms 121:4 Behold, He Who keeps Israel Will neither slumber nor sleep.

Psalms 121:5 The LORD is your keeper; the LORD is your shade on your right hand;

Psalms 121:6 The sun will not smite you by day, Nor the moon by night.

Psalms 121:7 The LORD will protect you from all evil; He will keep your soul.

Psalms 121:8 The Lord will guard your going out and your coming in From this time forth and forever. (NASB)

FLCR FACTS

I look up and wonder where my help will come from.

My help comes from God who made heaven and earth

God won't let me fall because He is always watching, He doesn't sleep

He keeps Israel and doesn't sleep or even slumber

The Lord keeps me and shades me at my right hand

The Lord protects me from evil He is keeping my soul safe

FLCR LESSONS

There are times we know we need help beyond ourselves

Help comes from God Who created heaven and earth and is alert and ready to help

God is constantly watching, ready to catch me before I fall

He can be so attentive because He never sleep or slumbers

God "keeps" Israel; God "keeps" me. Keeping me means He observes me, guards me, takes care of me, maintains me, retains me in His possession.

FLCR CHALLENGES

Am I humble enough to seek help when I need it?

Do I go to God for help, or something else?

Do I trust God to "keep" me?

Am I willing to learn what God considers "falling" instead of assuming falling means failure.

FLCR RESPONSES

Lord, help me to be more aware of Your help and presence.

Help me see my relationship with You from Your perspective.

*"God
does what is right,
but that doesn't mean
we will."*

the Authors

Passage 1:
Able ~ Murdered For His Faith

In the three chapters before this passage, God created the world and all that is in it. He provided the perfect Garden of Eden where everything you could want was freely available and He placed Adam and Eve in it. God only gave one restriction and Satan succeeded in focusing their attention on that restriction and getting them to violate it. When they violated it they started their mortality clock ticking, plunged the world into sin, and got kicked out of the Garden of Eden. As our passage opens Adam and Eve are adjusting to being out of the Garden of Eden and are setting out to make a life for themselves.

As you *FLCR* the passage you may wonder what made Abel's sacrifice better than Cain's. Try not to dwell on this too much. In the end the text says God thought it was better and if you can accept His appraisal without questioning it, you are in a better position to learn from the rest of the passage. However, if you want to wrestle with it, the answer revolves around the following words—the words that describe Cain's offering in verse 3 *("an offering")*, the words that describe Abel's offering in verse 4 *("of the firstlings…of their fat portions")* and the words that interpret Abel's offering in *Hebrews 11:4 ("by faith….")*.

Since this is a longer passage, you will want to divide it up into sections. I [N] suggest dividing it into three sections: *Genesis 4:1-8, Genesis 4:9-17,* and *Hebrews 11:4.* Read one section completely then write *FLCR* statements on it. Then go to the next section and do the same.

Do not neglect *verse 7*. It is one of the greatest verses for spiritual life guidance. Do not miss how God's punishment of Cain in the second section is also accompanied by kindness. What kind of person accompanies punishment with kindness? And also look at what Adam and Eve might learn from these events.

Genesis 4:1 Now the man had relations with his wife Eve, and she conceived and gave birth to Cain, and she said, "I have gotten a manchild with [the help of] the LORD."

Genesis 4:2 Again, she gave birth to his brother Abel. And Abel was a keeper of flocks, but Cain was a tiller of the ground.

Genesis 4:3 So it came about in the course of time that Cain brought an offering to the LORD of the fruit of the ground.

Genesis 4:4 Abel, on his part also brought of the firstlings of his flock and of their fat portions. And the LORD had regard for Abel and for his offering;

Genesis 4:5 but for Cain and for his offering He had no regard. So Cain became very angry and his countenance fell.

Genesis 4:6 Then the LORD said to Cain, "Why are you angry? And why has your countenance fallen?

Genesis 4:7 "If you do well, will not [your countenance] be lifted up? And if you do not do well, sin is crouching at the door; and its desire is for you, but you must master it."

Genesis 4:8 Cain told Abel his brother. And it came about when they were in the field, that Cain rose up against Abel his brother and killed him.

Genesis 4:9 Then the LORD said to Cain, "Where is Abel your brother?" And he said, "I do not know. Am I my brother's keeper?"

Genesis 4:10 He said, "What have you done? The voice of your brother's blood is crying to Me from the ground.

Genesis 4:11 "Now you are cursed from the ground, which has opened its mouth to receive your brother's blood from your hand.

Genesis 4:12 "When you cultivate the ground, it will no longer yield its strength to you; you will be a vagrant and a wanderer on the earth."

Genesis 4:13 Cain said to the LORD, "My punishment is too great to bear!

Passage 1—Hebrews 11:4

Genesis 4:14 "Behold, You have driven me this day from the face of the ground; and from Your face I will be hidden, and I will be a vagrant and a wanderer on the earth, and whoever finds me will kill me."

Genesis 4:15 So the LORD said to him, "Therefore whoever kills Cain, vengeance will be taken on him sevenfold." And the LORD appointed a sign for Cain, so that no one finding him would slay him.

Genesis 4:16 Then Cain went out from the presence of the LORD, and settled in the land of Nod, east of Eden.

Genesis 4:17 Cain had relations with his wife and she conceived, and gave birth to Enoch; and he built a city, and called the name of the city Enoch, after the name of his son.

...

Hebrews 11:4 By faith Abel offered to God a better sacrifice than Cain, through which he obtained the testimony that he was righteous, God testifying about his gifts, and through faith, though he is dead, he still speaks. (NASB1995)

FLCR FACTS

Adam had relations with his wife Eve.

It can look like evil triumphs sometimes.

FLCR CHALLENGES

Do I believe that God is just and will triumph in the end?

FLCR RESPONSES

Commentary

I [D] wonder what it was like for Adam and Eve raising their first children? There is a chance that Cain and Abel were twins because there is no time interval mentioned between their births. Twins or not, things started out so well. Eve gave God the credit for creating her male child. How could things go so wrong when God was involved?

It can be very disheartening when it looks like evil triumphs. God allowed Cain to overpower and kill Abel. Adam and Eve must have been devastated. Their righteous son murdered by their angry son. Abel was murdered for his faith in the God who provided for him.

Why would God allow evil to triumph? In times like these it is important to remember that God gives all of us the freedom to choose. Adam and Eve could have done a perfect job as diligent, loving parents and still not turned out a god-fearing, loving, responsible child. Welcome to God's world.

God does what is right but that doesn't mean we will. We all have choices. As parents we only control the child's home environment, but there are two other key influences. Genetics determines our child's personality predispositions toward anger, anxiety, submission and a myriad of other factors. Add your child's own will to choose for themselves and that gives parents only a third of the controlling factors for how things turn out. God seems to rate our ability to choose to do right as very important. I guess He didn't want little robots obeying Him because they have no choice. It is much more fun to have children who choose to obey you because they respect and love you.

God has a bigger perspective. This story did not end with Cain prevailing over Abel. Consider that Abel has been famous for centuries because of his faith-filled offering. He is the one who triumphs. He has inspired many to follow his example of gratefully giving back to God.

God makes a point of saying it was Abel's faith that made him righteous. His offering (i.e. his works) did not save him. His good offering flowed from his good faith and gratitude for the God who provides. God's plan of salvation has always been about faith in Him and His provision.

Even from the beginning, God wanted His children to know that He is the One who provides, but we are the ones who are responsible to put our faith in Him and be vigilant to master sin.

What God Is Like

- *1. God values our freedom to choose.* He does not want to over-control us so that we have no choice. He wants a real relationship where we choose thankfulness, obedience, humility, love and respect. We are equipped to master sin by choosing to do the right thing, even if it's after choosing to do the wrong thing.

- *2. God is a proud Father.* He talks about our good behavior. He testifies about Abel's offering of faith and allows his faith to testify even though he has been dead for centuries.

- *3. God is humble.* He does not require that everyone continually glorify Him. He parents us perfectly, but we can choose to thwart His efforts to make us righteous. He is willing to not be glorified for a time in order to find real relationships with His children.

- *4. God does not change.* He has always saved His children by their faith in Him.

- *5. God spends time to teach His children.* He wants to help us. God had taught Cain and Abel how to present an offering because Abel knew what to do. God was willing to take time and instruct Cain on the danger of sin and his responsibility to master it, even when Cain had ignored His previous instructions.

*"Our sin does not
control God
and His holiness,
but it sure can
control us."*

the Authors

Passage 2:
Sarah ~ One Who Had Wavering Faith

Abraham and Sarah were childless for a long while. During that time God promised to make a great nation out of Abraham (*Genesis 12:1-2*). When God made that promise Abraham was 75 years old.

God repeats the promise in *Genesis 13:16* saying He would make Abraham's descendants more numerous than the *"dust of the earth"*—that's a lot of descendants. However, as our passage opens it is 24 years after the second promise, Abraham is now 99 years old which was beyond childbearing years, and he still does not have any children. By way of comparison, people lived longer back then and Abraham died when he was 175 years old.

This present passage explores the question, "What do you do when God's will is taking too long?"

The passage divides nicely into three parts. In *Genesis 16:1-6* Abraham and Sarah get tired of waiting and take action. In *Genesis 18:10-15* God reiterates His promise and gives a time frame. In *Hebrews 11:11* God gives us His overall take on Sarah's faith in His promise.

As you *FLCR* this passage make sure to notice what Abraham and Sarah do when their patience for God's timing wears thin. Did their actions change God's promise?

Consider how long they had to wait to receive a very real and specific promise that God had made. Can waiting be part of God's plan? Are we prepared to wait if need be?

Also ponder the question, *"Is anything too difficult for the LORD?"* (*Genesis 18:14*)

Passage 2—Genesis 16:1-6;18:1,10-15

Genesis 16:1 Now Sarai, Abram's wife had borne him no [children,] and she had an Egyptian maid whose name was Hagar.

Genesis 16:2 So Sarai said to Abram, "Now behold, the LORD has prevented me from bearing [children.] Please go in to my maid; perhaps I will obtain children through her." And Abram listened to the voice of Sarai.

Genesis 16:3 After Abram had lived ten years in the land of Canaan, Abram's wife Sarai took Hagar the Egyptian, her maid, and gave her to her husband Abram as his wife.

Genesis 16:4 He went in to Hagar, and she conceived; and when she saw that she had conceived, her mistress was despised in her sight.

Genesis 16:5 And Sarai said to Abram, "May the wrong done me be upon you. I gave my maid into your arms, but when she saw that she had conceived, I was despised in her sight. May the LORD judge between you and me."

Genesis 16:6 But Abram said to Sarai, "Behold, your maid is in your power; do to her what is good in your sight." So Sarai treated her harshly, and she fled from her presence. (NASB1995)

...

Genesis 18:1 Now the LORD appeared to him by the oaks of Mamre, while he was sitting at the tent door in the heat of the day. (NASB1995)

...

Genesis 18:10 He said, "I will surely return to you at this time next year; and behold, Sarah your wife will have a son." And Sarah was listening at the tent door, which was behind him.

Genesis 18:11 Now Abraham and Sarah were old, advanced in age; Sarah was past childbearing.

Genesis 18:12 Sarah laughed to herself, saying, "After I have become old, shall I have pleasure, my lord being old also?"

Genesis 18:13 And the LORD said to Abraham, "Why did Sarah laugh, saying, 'Shall I indeed bear [a child,] when I am [so] old?'

Passage 2—Hebrews 11:11

Genesis 18:14 "Is anything too difficult for the LORD? At the appointed time I will return to you, at this time next year, and Sarah will have a son."

Genesis 18:15 Sarah denied [it] however, saying, "I did not laugh"; for she was afraid. And He said, "No, but you did laugh." (NASB1995)

...

Hebrews 11:11 By faith even Sarah herself received ability to conceive, even beyond the proper time of life, since she considered Him faithful who had promised. (NASB1995)

FLCR FACTS

Sarai, Abram's wife, was childless with Abram.

The Lord prevents and enables conception for His own reasons. The timing of Sarai's conception was "appointed."

FLCR CHALLENGES

Do I believe that God prevents and enables conception for good reasons?

FLCR RESPONSES

Commentary

God is not "co-dependent." He did not keep Hagar from conceiving in order to control Abraham and Sarah's sin (i.e. Abram and Sarai's sin). But their sin hurt Hagar.

God had a benevolent reason to prevent Sarah and Abraham from conceiving, but He had not placed that limitation on Hagar. Hagar was under Abraham and Sarah's authority, and they abused their power over her. When we give up and assume God is not going to fulfill His promises in our life, we are more likely to take matters into our own hands and get off track. Our impatient solutions usually hurt others and ourselves. But, God keeps His promises, even when we sin. Our sin does not control Him and His holiness, but it sure can control us. We can end up in a mess.

Abraham and Sarah might have ended up with a baby, but they had a war in their home. Sarah blamed Abraham, Hagar despised Sarah, and it all boiled down to them not waiting for God. It is hard to wait for years, but if we abuse our power and "force things to happen" chances are, things will get worse. If we abuse our power and cause someone else to sin they will resent us.

It is difficult for some personalities to accept responsibility for their sin. Those kind look to blame other people. Sarah blamed both Abraham and Hagar when her plan went south. After Sarah denied laughing at God's promise of a son, the Lord not only stated the truth of her disbelief, but also taught her the right attitude—"Is anything too difficult for the Lord?" She needed to spend less time blaming and more time being honest with God about her sin.

If God asks you to wait years to fulfill a promise, it becomes a test. Do you trust that God will keep His promise, or do you give up and take matters into your own hands? It boils down to "who is in charge of my life—God or me?" Our big challenge is to humbly live our life depending on God and His timing. When we bolt from humbly waiting on God we complicate our life. Believing God knows best, and being willing to follow Him is the challenge of our life. Things work out for those who wait on Him.

I think most of us know what it looks like when we don't wait. But, how do you know if you are waiting appropriately or inappropriately? Our clue comes from our attitude and actions. If we are exercising faith and doing our part while letting God do His part, we are probably waiting appropriately. But, if we are passively waiting for God to do it all, we are probably waiting inappropriately.

Sarah and Abraham still needed to do their part—they still needed have sexual relations. Their relations are an act of faith in His ability to fulfill His promise. If they stopped relating and said getting pregnant was all up to God, they would not be waiting appropriately. While we wait, our job is to continue to do our part, expecting that God will do His part in His time.

It is encouraging to see how graciously God summarizes Sarah's life in *Hebrews 11:11*. He did not focus on her doubtful moments. He attributed the power to conceive as coming from her faith. We might be feeble and fail, but God loves and remembers our faith.

What God Is Like

- *1. God wants a "real" relationship with us.* He wants us to be honest with Him so He can help us. He wanted Sarai to be honest with Him. When she wasn't, He offered His help anyway.

- *2. God is always good and faithful, even when we are not.*

- *3. God has definite appointments and timetables for each of us.* He is active in the plan for our life.

- *4. God does not have the same plan for every child.* Hagar got pregnant easily. Sarai was unable to get pregnant for most of her life. Both women were loved by God.

- *5. God is confident of His ability.* He knows nothing is too difficult for Him.

*"God
uses us
as we are."*

the Authors

Passage 3

Passage 3:
Rahab ~ An Unlikely Ally

God promised to make Abraham a great nation and give them a land and a blessing *(Genesis 12:1-3)*. As this passage opens Abraham's descendants are known as the children of Israel (Israel is Abraham's grandson) and Joshua is their leader. God is about to give them the land of Canaan and has commissioned Joshua to lead the people into the land and to take the land by force knowing that He has given it to them. Joshua's first order of business is to send 2 spies to Jericho, the first town in the land, to gather the information needed for their battle.

This passage is fairly long and divides into three parts:

- Rahab hides the spies (Joshua 2:1-7),

- Rahab requests protection (Joshua 2:8-13),

- The spies agree and take an oath (Joshua 2:14-21).

I {N} would suggest that you read the first section, write about five or six *Facts* and one or two *Lessons* and *Challenges* then go on to the next sections and do the same. The answers in the back include more *FLCR* statements which are provided to give you more samples to learn from. We don't expect you to come up with that many statements.

As you start studying these longer passages, the new skill is to get *Facts, Lessons,* and *Challenges* from larger sections (several verses) at a time. You are enlarging the segment of the passage that you are looking at for your *Facts* etc.

The glaring problem in the passage is that God is blessing the telling of lies to the authorities. As always, you will get more out of this passage by spending little or no time on this problem. But if you do chase it, *begin* with the idea that God *is* blessing it, and come up with reasons why He might do that in this case.

Joshua 2:1 Then Joshua the son of Nun sent two men as spies secretly from Shittim, saying, "Go, view the land, especially Jericho." So they went and came into the house of a harlot whose name was Rahab, and lodged there.

Joshua 2:2 It was told the king of Jericho, saying, "Behold, men from the sons of Israel have come here tonight to search out the land."

Joshua 2:3 And the king of Jericho sent [word] to Rahab, saying, "Bring out the men who have come to you, who have entered your house, for they have come to search out all the land."

Joshua 2:4 But the woman had taken the two men and hidden them, and she said, "Yes, the men came to me, but I did not know where they were from.

Joshua 2:5 "It came about when [it was time] to shut the gate at dark, that the men went out; I do not know where the men went. Pursue them quickly, for you will overtake them."

Joshua 2:6 But she had brought them up to the roof and hidden them in the stalks of flax which she had laid in order on the roof.

Joshua 2:7 So the men pursued them on the road to the Jordan to the fords; and as soon as those who were pursuing them had gone out, they shut the gate.

Joshua 2:8 Now before they lay down, she came up to them on the roof,

Joshua 2:9 and said to the men, "I know that the LORD has given you the land, and that the terror of you has fallen on us, and that all the inhabitants of the land have melted away before you.

Joshua 2:10 "For we have heard how the LORD dried up the water of the Red Sea before you when you came out of Egypt, and what you did to the two kings of the Amorites who were beyond the Jordan, to Sihon and Og, whom you utterly destroyed.

Joshua 2:11 "When we heard [it,] our hearts melted and no courage remained in any man any longer because of you; for the LORD your God, He is God in heaven above and on earth beneath.

Joshua 2:12 "Now therefore, please swear to me by the LORD, since I have dealt kindly with you, that you also will deal kindly with my father's household, and give me a pledge of truth,

Joshua 2:13 and spare my father and my mother and my brothers and my sisters, with all who belong to them, and deliver our lives from death."

Joshua 2:14 So the men said to her, "Our life for yours if you do not tell this business of ours; and it shall come about when the LORD gives us the land that we will deal kindly and faithfully with you."

Joshua 2:15 Then she let them down by a rope through the window, for her house was on the city wall, so that she was living on the wall.

Joshua 2:16 She said to them, "Go to the hill country, so that the pursuers will not happen upon you, and hide yourselves there for three days until the pursuers return. Then afterward you may go on your way."

Joshua 2:17 The men said to her, "We [shall be] free from this oath to you which you have made us swear,

Joshua 2:18 unless, when we come into the land, you tie this cord of scarlet thread in the window through which you let us down, and gather to yourself into the house your father and your mother and your brothers and all your father's household.

Joshua 2:19 "It shall come about that anyone who goes out of the doors of your house into the street, his blood [shall be] on his own head, and we [shall be] free; but anyone who is with you in the house, his blood [shall be] on our head if a hand is [laid] on him.

Joshua 2:20 "But if you tell this business of ours, then we shall be free from the oath which you have made us swear."

Joshua 2:21 She said, "According to your words, so be it." So she sent them away, and they departed; and she tied the scarlet cord in the window. (NASB1995)

...

Hebrews 11:31 By faith Rahab the harlot did not perish along with those who were disobedient, after she had welcomed the spies in peace. (NASB1995)

FLCR FACTS

Rahab was a harlot.

God uses unlikely people for His purposes. Rahab had morality issues, but she had faith in the God of Israel as the true God in heaven and on earth. God used her for His purposes.

FLCR CHALLENGES

Do I focus on myself and think I need to be sinless before God will use me?

FLCR RESPONSES

Commentary

God has used some unlikely people in my [D] life. How about you? The spies set out for Jericho and end up being helped by a harlot. If I was God, that's not how I would script it. Fortunately for everyone, I'm not God.

God looks at the heart. He saw Rahab's faith and reverential fear and that was more important to Him than her sin. Rahab had morality issues, but her new faith in the God of Israel as the true God of heaven and earth aligned her with His purposes. Notice that God did not wait until she was sinless. If He did that He would never be able to use any of us. God uses us as we are.

Rahab lied to protect the spies and God overlooked this because of her new faith and fear of Him. She was cooperating with His purposes.

Rahab was focused on God, not herself. She did not say, "I can't help because I'm a harlot, I need to clean up my life first." She jumped right in because she feared the God of Israel and wanted to get on His side. Yes, her choice saved her life, but she was choosing to follow the One true God— that was her focus. The longer a person walks with God and focuses on Him, the less morality issues we will have, but Rahab was new to her faith and God used her as she was.

God also doesn't seem to mind His children being shrewd and negotiating deals to accomplish His will. He seems to bless those who get past their fear and act in obedience to His will. Since God was calling them into enemy territory the spies needed to believe that He could lead them through to safety. So they listened to and followed, Rahab's advice. They weren't too proud to be helped by a woman of low social standing. On the other hand, the reason Rahab was willing to face her fear of being caught by the King of Jericho was because she feared the God of Israel more. God honors faith and used this unlikely alliance in order to save the spies and a harlot who feared Him. There is a chance that Rahab might have been disrespected by her family and culture because of her work, but in the end, she was wiser than all of them.

If God calls you to go into enemy territory do you believe He can lead you through to safety? Would you be willing to receive help from some unlikely people? We tend to want to surround ourselves with people like us. We might miss out on some amazing liaisons if we are too rigid. God looks at the heart. We need to look to God. It is safer to fear Him than the danger.

What God Is Like

- *1. God is impressed with faith and reverential fear.* He not only saved Rahab and her family because of her faith, but He honors her *(Hebrews 11:31).*

- *2. God is generous.* He saved all of Rahab's family from certain death, based on her faith alone.

- *3. God wants us to trust Him.* He puts His children in situations that demand faith in Him.

- *4. God performs miracles not just for the ones receiving the miracle, but for unbelievers watching.* Rahab heard about God's miracles for the Israelites. Many saw, but she believed and turned to Him.

"God rewarded her
with
four sons and
two daughters."

the Authors

Passage 4:
Hannah ~ God Uses The Humble

Waiting on God is always difficult but this passage shows us someone who found a way to wait successfully and was rewarded for it.

As the passage opens, the nation of Israel is living in the land of Palestine (which God gave to them) and is being led by the Priests who are descendants of Israel's son Levi. This is before the nation had a king and they were technically organized as a *theocracy*— people who are being led directly by God through His Priests. Currently the Priesthood is suffering under the weight of wicked Priests and the passage describes how Samuel rose up to became a great Priest and restored godly leadership in the nation Israel.

Remember how I [N] said these passages will help teach you how to *FLCR* longer passages? Well, buckle up, this is the longest passage in the book. It is helpful to divid it into these sections.

- Hannah Is Barren And Distressed By It *(1 Samuel 1:1-8)*.
- Hannah Makes A Vow To God (1 Samuel 1:9-19).
- God Gives Hannah A Son, Hannah Gives God A Priest *(1 Samuel 1:20-28)*.
- Hannah Praises God *(1 Samuel 2:1-11)*.

Address the long sections by making *summary FLCR* statements. Here are some example *Facts:* "Hannah was barren," "She was ridiculed," "But her husband supported her." *FLCR* each section using *summary* statements like these.

In her culture being barren was viewed as being less than adequate. Can you relate with Hannah's dilemma and learn from how she chooses to deal with it? Besides identifying with her hardships, also learn from the ways she was strong and grateful. From your point of view, was her sacrifice worth it?

Passage 4—1 Samuel 1:1-2:12

1 Samuel 1:1 Now there was a certain man from Ramathaim-zophim from the hill country of Ephraim, and his name was Elkanah the son of Jeroham, the son of Elihu, the son of Tohu, the son of Zuph, an Ephraimite.

1 Samuel 1:2 He had two wives: the name of one was Hannah and the name of the other Peninnah; and Peninnah had children, but Hannah had no children.

1 Samuel 1:3 Now this man would go up from his city yearly to worship and to sacrifice to the LORD of hosts in Shiloh. And the two sons of Eli, Hophni and Phinehas, were priests to the LORD there.

1 Samuel 1:4 When the day came that Elkanah sacrificed, he would give portions to Peninnah his wife and to all her sons and her daughters;

1 Samuel 1:5 but to Hannah he would give a double portion, for he loved Hannah, but the LORD had closed her womb.

1 Samuel 1:6 Her rival, however, would provoke her bitterly to irritate her, because the LORD had closed her womb.

1 Samuel 1:7 It happened year after year, as often as she went up to the house of the LORD, she would provoke her; so she wept and would not eat.

1 Samuel 1:8 Then Elkanah her husband said to her, "Hannah, why do you weep and why do you not eat and why is your heart sad? Am I not better to you than ten sons?"

1 Samuel 1:9 Then Hannah rose after eating and drinking in Shiloh. Now Eli the priest was sitting on the seat by the doorpost of the temple of the LORD.

1 Samuel 1:10 She, greatly distressed, prayed to the LORD and wept bitterly.

1 Samuel 1:11 She made a vow and said, "O LORD of hosts, if You will indeed look on the affliction of Your maidservant and remember me, and not forget Your maidservant, but will give Your maidservant a son, then I will give him to the LORD all the days of his life, and a razor shall never come on his head."

Passage 4—1 Samuel 1:1-2:12

1 Samuel 1:12 Now it came about, as she continued praying before the LORD, that Eli was watching her mouth.

1 Samuel 1:13 As for Hannah, she was speaking in her heart, only her lips were moving, but her voice was not heard. So Eli thought she was drunk.

1 Samuel 1:14 Then Eli said to her, "How long will you make yourself drunk? Put away your wine from you."

1 Samuel 1:15 But Hannah replied, "No, my lord, I am a woman oppressed in spirit; I have drunk neither wine nor strong drink, but I have poured out my soul before the LORD.

1 Samuel 1:16 "Do not consider your maidservant as a worthless woman, for I have spoken until now out of my great concern and provocation."

1 Samuel 1:17 Then Eli answered and said, "Go in peace; and may the God of Israel grant your petition that you have asked of Him."

1 Samuel 1:18 She said, "Let your maidservant find favor in your sight." So the woman went her way and ate, and her face was no longer [sad.]

1 Samuel 1:19 Then they arose early in the morning and worshiped before the LORD, and returned again to their house in Ramah. And Elkanah had relations with Hannah his wife, and the LORD remembered her.

1 Samuel 1:20 It came about in due time, after Hannah had conceived, that she gave birth to a son; and she named him Samuel, [saying,] "Because I have asked him of the LORD."

1 Samuel 1:21 Then the man Elkanah went up with all his household to offer to the LORD the yearly sacrifice and [pay] his vow.

1 Samuel 1:22 But Hannah did not go up, for she said to her husband, "[I will not go up] until the child is weaned; then I will bring him, that he may appear before the LORD and stay there forever."

1 Samuel 1:23 Elkanah her husband said to her, "Do what seems best to you. Remain until you have weaned him; only may the LORD confirm His word." So the woman remained and nursed her son until she weaned him.

1 Samuel 1:24 Now when she had weaned him, she took him up with her, with a three-year-old bull and one ephah of flour and a jug of wine, and brought him to the house of the LORD in Shiloh, although the child was young.

1 Samuel 1:25 Then they slaughtered the bull, and brought the boy to Eli.

1 Samuel 1:26 She said, "Oh, my lord! As your soul lives, my lord, I am the woman who stood here beside you, praying to the LORD.

1 Samuel 1:27 "For this boy I prayed, and the LORD has given me my petition which I asked of Him.

1 Samuel 1:28 "So I have also dedicated him to the LORD; as long as he lives he is dedicated to the LORD." And he worshiped the LORD there.

1 Samuel 2:1 Then Hannah prayed and said, "My heart exults in the LORD; My horn is exalted in the LORD, My mouth speaks boldly against my enemies, Because I rejoice in Your salvation.

1 Samuel 2:2 "There is no one holy like the LORD, Indeed, there is no one besides You, Nor is there any rock like our God.

1 Samuel 2:3 "Boast no more so very proudly, Do not let arrogance come out of your mouth; For the LORD is a God of knowledge, And with Him actions are weighed.

1 Samuel 2:4 "The bows of the mighty are shattered, But the feeble gird on strength.

1 Samuel 2:5 "Those who were full hire themselves out for bread, But those who were hungry cease [to hunger.] Even the barren gives birth to seven, But she who has many children languishes.

1 Samuel 2:6 "The LORD kills and makes alive; He brings down to Sheol and raises up.

Passage 4—1 Samuel 1:1-2:12

1 Samuel 2:7 "The LORD makes poor and rich; He brings low, He also exalts.

1 Samuel 2:8 "He raises the poor from the dust, He lifts the needy from the ash heap To make them sit with nobles, And inherit a seat of honor; For the pillars of the earth are the LORD'S, And He set the world on them.

1 Samuel 2:9 "He keeps the feet of His godly ones, But the wicked ones are silenced in darkness; For not by might shall a man prevail.

1 Samuel 2:10 "Those who contend with the LORD will be shattered; Against them He will thunder in the heavens, The LORD will judge the ends of the earth; And He will give strength to His king, And will exalt the horn of His anointed."

1 Samuel 2:11 Then Elkanah went to his home at Ramah. But the boy ministered to the LORD before Eli the priest.

1 Samuel 2:12 Now the sons of Eli were worthless men; they did not know the LORD (NASB1995)

FLCR FACTS

A man from Ephraim named Elkanah, son of Jeroham had two wives.

Our desperation can be an answer to God.

FLCR CHALLENGES

Do I realize my needs might have a purpose for God?

FLCR RESPONSES

Commentary

Imagine Hannah's situation. Year after year Peninnah made her feel inferior. Hannah might have worried that God agreed. So she poured out her heart to God in prayer and the priest, God's "representative," accused her of being a drunk "worthless woman." Yikes! That's a lot of pain. She could have left in an angry huff. Instead, she humbly explained her situation to the priest. Her humble reaction helped the priest change his mind and intercede for her. Her situation had not changed. She was still childless, but she left supported by the priest and full of hope.

Hannah did many things right during her barren years. She kept worshipping. She kept praying. She did not give up on God. Instead, she adjusted her request. She had been asking for a son, but now she promised to give her son to God. Apparently that was what God was waiting for, because He granted her request. She trusted God enough to give Him what she considered her best. She gave her son over to God with generosity and gratitude of heart.

Hannah kept her promise, but she kept it her way with poise and trust in God. She did not feel the need to give Samuel over to the priest before he was weaned. She did not fear God's wrath when she stayed home from their yearly trip to the temple. She was confident of her commitment and confident of God's love. Her husband's trust in her character and judgment must have been rewarding.

Hannah shared her real emotions with God. She wept, mourned, and worshipped Him in the barren times and she rejoiced in Him in the abundant times. She did not focus on the blessings, but her rejoicing was in Him. Hannah kept worshipping through the hard times which helped her focus and worship Him in the good times.

For years things looked very bleak for Hannah. She was childless in a culture that assumed being barren was a curse from God. She gave God her best and He rewarded her with four sons and two daughters. She may have wondered at times if God loved her, but He had bigger plans for Hannah than she could imagine. All He needed was her best, which she gave, and God has made her and her son, famous to this day. I'm sure it was a marvelous blessing to have three other sons and two daughters, but what she gave to God was blessed the most. God allowed her to have barren times in order to prepare her to receive His blessings.

Everything that happens to us is preparation for something else. Will we adapt and give God our best even when it hurts?

What God Is Like

- *1. God is incredibly generous.* You can't out-give Him. Hannah gave God her best and He responded by blessing her with fame, a son used mightily by Him, and 3 other sons and 2 daughters.

- *2. God can use suffering.* He allows us to have barren times in order to prepare us to receive His best blessings.

- *3. God is sovereign over all.* He makes rich or poor. He exalts and brings low. He gives life and kills. He gives strength to the weak and defeats the mighty. We only succeed because He enables us to succeed. He is working closely in everyone's life.

- *4. God protects His godly ones.* He cares about His children. Evil might try to kill His children, but God guards our souls so nothing can separate us from Him.

*"Environment
is not the only element
that determines
a child's outcome."*

the Authors

Passage 5:
Samuel ~ God Uses The Sincere

When you have a crisis in leadership everybody suffers. This passage describes how God purified the leadership of the children of Israel through the godly Priest Samuel.

There are two topics covered in this passage. First, the wickedness and judgement of the corrupt Priests (mentioned in verse *(2:12)* and elaborated in *(3:12-18))*. Second, the rise of the godly Priest Samuel (described in all the other verses). During this time period the nation of Israel was directly connected to God by the Priests. Since there was no King, the Priests were leading the nation. Removing wicked Priests and installing godly Priests was crucial to the proper functioning of this *theocratic* nation.

I would *FLCR* these two sections individually and watch how God is not willing to let sin take over the religious leadership of His people and how He raises up and installs a godly leader.

As we will mention in the commentary, parents don't have complete control over how their kids turn out. Can you see why God was upset over what Eli did with his small amount of influence over his kids?

Pay particular attention to the description of Samuel's dream in verses *(3:1-18)*. There are many things that can be learned in this section about how God communicates with us and how we can make ourselves ready to receive a message from God.

Passage 5—1 Samuel 2:12, 18-21, 34-36, 3:1-21

1 Samuel 2:12 Now the sons of Eli were worthless men; they did not know the LORD

...

1 Samuel 2:18 Now Samuel was ministering before the LORD, [as] a boy wearing a linen ephod.

1 Samuel 2:19 And his mother would make him a little robe and bring it to him from year to year when she would come up with her husband to offer the yearly sacrifice.

1 Samuel 2:20 Then Eli would bless Elkanah and his wife and say, "May the LORD give you children from this woman in place of the one she dedicated to the LORD." And they went to their own home.

1 Samuel 2:21 The LORD visited Hannah; and she conceived and gave birth to three sons and two daughters. And the boy Samuel grew before the LORD.

...

1 Samuel 2:34 'This will be the sign to you which will come concerning your two sons, Hophni and Phinehas: on the same day both of them will die.

1 Samuel 2:35 'But I will raise up for Myself a faithful priest who will do according to what is in My heart and in My soul; and I will build him an enduring house, and he will walk before My anointed always.

1 Samuel 2:36 'Everyone who is left in your house will come and bow down to him for a piece of silver or a loaf of bread and say, "Please assign me to one of the priest's offices so that I may eat a piece of bread."'"

1 Samuel 3:1 Now the boy Samuel was ministering to the LORD before Eli. And word from the LORD was rare in those days, visions were infrequent.

1 Samuel 3:2 It happened at that time as Eli was lying down in his place (now his eyesight had begun to grow dim [and] he could not see [well]),]

1 Samuel 3:3 and the lamp of God had not yet gone out, and Samuel was lying down in the temple of the LORD where the ark of God [was,]

Passage 5—1 Samuel 2:12, 18-21, 34-36, 3:1-21

1 Samuel 3:4 that the LORD called Samuel; and he said, "Here I am."

1 Samuel 3:5 Then he ran to Eli and said, "Here I am, for you called me." But he said, "I did not call, lie down again." So he went and lay down.

1 Samuel 3:6 The LORD called yet again, "Samuel!" So Samuel arose and went to Eli and said, "Here I am, for you called me." But he answered, "I did not call, my son, lie down again."

1 Samuel 3:7 Now Samuel did not yet know the LORD, nor had the word of the LORD yet been revealed to him.

1 Samuel 3:8 So the LORD called Samuel again for the third time. And he arose and went to Eli and said, "Here I am, for you called me." Then Eli discerned that the LORD was calling the boy.

1 Samuel 3:9 And Eli said to Samuel, "Go lie down, and it shall be if He calls you, that you shall say, 'Speak, LORD, for Your servant is listening.'" So Samuel went and lay down in his place.

1 Samuel 3:10 Then the LORD came and stood and called as at other times, "Samuel! Samuel!" And Samuel said, "Speak, for Your servant is listening."

1 Samuel 3:11 The LORD said to Samuel, "Behold, I am about to do a thing in Israel at which both ears of everyone who hears it will tingle.

1 Samuel 3:12 "In that day I will carry out against Eli all that I have spoken concerning his house, from beginning to end.

1 Samuel 3:13 "For I have told him that I am about to judge his house forever for the iniquity which he knew, because his sons brought a curse on themselves and he did not rebuke them.

1 Samuel 3:14 "Therefore I have sworn to the house of Eli that the iniquity of Eli's house shall not be atoned for by sacrifice or offering forever."

1 Samuel 3:15 So Samuel lay down until morning. Then he opened the doors of the house of the LORD. But Samuel was afraid to tell the vision to Eli.

1 Samuel 3:16 Then Eli called Samuel and said, "Samuel, my son." And he said, "Here I am."

Passage 5—1 Samuel 2:12, 18-21, 34-36, 3:1-21

1 Samuel 3:17 He said, "What is the word that He spoke to you? Please do not hide it from me. May God do so to you, and more also, if you hide anything from me of all the words that He spoke to you."

1 Samuel 3:18 So Samuel told him everything and hid nothing from him. And he said, "It is the LORD; let Him do what seems good to Him."

1 Samuel 3:19 Thus Samuel grew and the LORD was with him and let none of his words fail.

1 Samuel 3:20 All Israel from Dan even to Beersheba knew that Samuel was confirmed as a prophet of the LORD.

1 Samuel 3:21 And the LORD appeared again at Shiloh, because the LORD revealed Himself to Samuel at Shiloh by the word of the LORD. (NASB1995)

FLCR FACTS

The boy Samuel was ministering to the LORD before Eli.

FLCR LESSONS

God wants us to care about His heart.

FLCR CHALLENGES

Do I care about God's heart?

FLCR RESPONSES

Commentary

Notice that Eli raised 3 boys: his own 2 sons and Samuel. All 3 boys were raised by the same person yet 2 of the boys turned out evil and 1 of the boys, Samuel, turned out godly. Children can choose to follow God in spite of their corrupt environment. Environment does not determine a child's outcome. Environment is only one of three things that influence a child's outcome.

Children are also influenced by their genetics. For example, are they impulsive, laid back, or easily anxious? Genetics has a lot to do with that. Taking responsibility for whatever "weak links" God has given us through our genetics is part of our assignment. Some will choose to take responsibility for those "weak links" and get better. Others will choose to blame people for their weaknesses.

The last influence that determines a child's outcome is the child's own choices. Some children from godly homes make bad choices, and end up destitute, while other children from ungodly homes follow God and make wise choices, having a blessed life. A child's choices strongly influences where they end up. Eli's two older sons made wicked choices but Samuel chose to serve God and God blessed him for that.

Although Hannah did not raise Samuel, her desire to have a child made her desperate. Our desperation can enable something God desires if we get creative and give up our rigid idea of what we think we need. Hannah desired children—God desired a faithful priest. When Hannah became desperate enough to modify her request and give her requested child to God to be a Priest, she entered God's sweet spot. God was patient enough to wait years for Samuel to grow up and serve Him as a faithful priest. Hannah was flexible enough to see the beauty of this arrangement for Samuel and for herself.

Sometimes we need to think creatively when we are not getting what we want, instead of just repeating our desperate but rigid demands. Our needs might have a purpose for God. After Hannah gave Samuel to God, God abundantly gave Hannah her original request for children.

We can learn from Eli. Eli and his two wicked sons teach us that God holds parents responsible for the children who are living at home and practicing blatant sins. Eli ignored his son's wicked behavior. We should never put our children's wicked behavior as more important than reverence and devotion for God. God wants us to care about His heart. Devotion to God takes first place over wicked children.

God is very generous with those who serve Him generously. As Samuel grew the LORD was with him. The LORD confided in him and his prophecies never failed.

At first, things looked bleak in Hannah's life. She didn't feel like God was blessing her. But, because of her revised prayer request, millions have been inspired by her story. We serve the same God and out of our desperation can come our biggest blessings.

What God Is Like

- *1. God is very patient.* He was willing to wait for Samuel to grow up to fill the need for a godly priest.

- *2. God is not mocked.* Eli's sons' behavior offended God and He warned Eli of coming judgement.

- *3. God is humble and willing to use the humble.* He used the child Samuel and his humble mother Hannah.

- *4. God leads us quietly.* He came to Samuel in the quiet of the night.

*"Abigail
worked
in tandem
with God."*

the Authors

Passage 6:
Abigail ~ One Who Was Married To A Fool

When you are not the one who is in charge and the people who are in charge are making a royal mess out of everything, you may wonder if there is anything that can be done? Can a subordinate head off a disaster that is brought about by the people in charge?

Believe it or not the answer is yes. Abigail did it.

At every turn in this passage you see Abigail put in danger by the bad decisions of her husband and how she used her influences and resources to head off calamity and restore order and peace to her household.

Notice how well she blended her trust and reliance in God with the shrewd use of the things within her power. Just because the good guys win in the end, don't miss how well designed each of her moves were. She didn't overthrow the person in power, she went right for the problem and worked to resolve it.

It would have been easy to yield to the overwhelming power of the forces against her. If you are out numbered and over powered it would be a mistake to assume there is nothing you can do to improve things. Play close attention to what she used her resources to do and what she relied on God to do.

Passage 6—1 Samuel 25:2-42

1 Samuel 25:2 Now [there was] a man in Maon whose business was in Carmel; and the man was very rich, and he had three thousand sheep and a thousand goats. And it came about while he was shearing his sheep in Carmel

1 Samuel 25:3 (now the man's name was Nabal, and his wife's name was Abigail. And the woman was intelligent and beautiful in appearance, but the man was harsh and evil in [his] dealings, and he was a Calebite),

1 Samuel 25:4 that David heard in the wilderness that Nabal was shearing his sheep.

1 Samuel 25:5 So David sent ten young men; and David said to the young men, "Go up to Carmel, visit Nabal and greet him in my name;

1 Samuel 25:6 and thus you shall say, 'Have a long life, peace be to you, and peace be to your house, and peace be to all that you have.

1 Samuel 25:7 'Now I have heard that you have shearers; now your shepherds have been with us and we have not insulted them, nor have they missed anything all the days they were in Carmel.

1 Samuel 25:8 'Ask your young men and they will tell you. Therefore let [my] young men find favor in your eyes, for we have come on a festive day. Please give whatever you find at hand to your servants and to your son David.'"

1 Samuel 25:9 When David's young men came, they spoke to Nabal according to all these words in David's name; then they waited.

1 Samuel 25:10 But Nabal answered David's servants and said, "Who is David? And who is the son of Jesse? There are many servants today who are each breaking away from his master.

1 Samuel 25:11 "Shall I then take my bread and my water and my meat that I have slaughtered for my shearers, and give it to men whose origin I do not know?"

1 Samuel 25:12 So David's young men retraced their way and went back; and they came and told him according to all these words.

1 Samuel 25:13 David said to his men, "Each [of you] gird on his sword." So each man girded on his sword. And David also girded on

his sword, and about four hundred men went up behind David while two hundred stayed with the baggage.

1 Samuel 25:14 But one of the young men told Abigail, Nabal's wife, saying, "Behold, David sent messengers from the wilderness to greet our master, and he scorned them.

1 Samuel 25:15 "Yet the men were very good to us, and we were not insulted, nor did we miss anything as long as we went about with them, while we were in the fields.

1 Samuel 25:16 "They were a wall to us both by night and by day, all the time we were with them tending the sheep.

1 Samuel 25:17 "Now therefore, know and consider what you should do, for evil is plotted against our master and against all his household; and he is such a worthless man that no one can speak to him."

1 Samuel 25:18 Then Abigail hurried and took two hundred [loaves] of bread and two jugs of wine and five sheep already prepared and five measures of roasted grain and a hundred clusters of raisins and two hundred cakes of figs, and loaded [them] on donkeys.

1 Samuel 25:19 She said to her young men, "Go on before me; behold, I am coming after you." But she did not tell her husband Nabal.

1 Samuel 25:20 It came about as she was riding on her donkey and coming down by the hidden part of the mountain, that behold, David and his men were coming down toward her; so she met them.

1 Samuel 25:21 Now David had said, "Surely in vain I have guarded all that this [man] has in the wilderness, so that nothing was missed of all that belonged to him; and he has returned me evil for good.

1 Samuel 25:22 "May God do so to the enemies of David, and more also, if by morning I leave [as much as] one male of any who belong to him."

1 Samuel 25:23 When Abigail saw David, she hurried and dismounted from her donkey, and fell on her face before David and bowed herself to the ground.

Passage 6—1 Samuel 25:2-42

1 Samuel 25:24 She fell at his feet and said, "On me alone, my lord, be the blame. And please let your maidservant speak to you, and listen to the words of your maidservant.

1 Samuel 25:25 "Please do not let my lord pay attention to this worthless man, Nabal, for as his name is, so is he. Nabal is his name and folly is with him; but I your maidservant did not see the young men of my lord whom you sent.

1 Samuel 25:26 "Now therefore, my lord, as the LORD lives, and as your soul lives, since the LORD has restrained you from shedding blood, and from avenging yourself by your own hand, now then let your enemies and those who seek evil against my lord, be as Nabal.

1 Samuel 25:27 "Now let this gift which your maidservant has brought to my lord be given to the young men who accompany my lord.

1 Samuel 25:28 "Please forgive the transgression of your maidservant; for the LORD will certainly make for my lord an enduring house, because my lord is fighting the battles of the LORD, and evil will not be found in you all your days.

1 Samuel 25:29 "Should anyone rise up to pursue you and to seek your life, then the life of my lord shall be bound in the bundle of the living with the LORD your God; but the lives of your enemies He will sling out as from the hollow of a sling.

1 Samuel 25:30 "And when the LORD does for my lord according to all the good that He has spoken concerning you, and appoints you ruler over Israel,

1 Samuel 25:31 this will not cause grief or a troubled heart to my lord, both by having shed blood without cause and by my lord having avenged himself. When the LORD deals well with my lord, then remember your maidservant."

1 Samuel 25:32 Then David said to Abigail, "Blessed be the LORD God of Israel, who sent you this day to meet me,

1 Samuel 25:33 and blessed be your discernment, and blessed be you, who have kept me this day from bloodshed and from avenging myself by my own hand.

1 Samuel 25:34 "Nevertheless, as the LORD God of Israel lives, who has restrained me from harming you, unless you had come quickly to meet me, surely there would not have been left to Nabal until the morning light [as much as] one male."

1 Samuel 25:35 So David received from her hand what she had brought him and said to her, "Go up to your house in peace. See, I have listened to you and granted your request."

1 Samuel 25:36 Then Abigail came to Nabal, and behold, he was holding a feast in his house, like the feast of a king. And Nabal's heart was merry within him, for he was very drunk; so she did not tell him anything at all until the morning light.

1 Samuel 25:37 But in the morning, when the wine had gone out of Nabal, his wife told him these things, and his heart died within him so that he became [as] a stone.

1 Samuel 25:38 About ten days later, the LORD struck Nabal and he died.

1 Samuel 25:39 When David heard that Nabal was dead, he said, "Blessed be the LORD, who has pleaded the cause of my reproach from the hand of Nabal and has kept back His servant from evil. The LORD has also returned the evildoing of Nabal on his own head." Then David sent a proposal to Abigail, to take her as his wife.

1 Samuel 25:40 When the servants of David came to Abigail at Carmel, they spoke to her, saying, "David has sent us to you to take you as his wife."

1 Samuel 25:41 She arose and bowed with her face to the ground and said, "Behold, your maidservant is a maid to wash the feet of my lord's servants."

1 Samuel 25:42 Then Abigail quickly arose, and rode on a donkey, with her five maidens who attended her; and she followed the messengers of David and became his wife. (NASB1995)

FLCR FACTS

A rich man came to Carmel on business.

God wants us to be generous with those in need.

FLCR CHALLENGES

When someone in need is kind to me am I generous in return?

FLCR RESPONSES

Commentary

If you heard that your spouse had been harsh and evil to someone and it incited them to bring evil vengeance against your household, what would you do? Would you indulge your fear and anger and take things out on your spouse? Or would you put 100% of the problem on God and wait for Him to fix it? Abigail prayed then sprang into action doing what her spouse should have done in the first place.

Abigail chose wisely. She worked in tandem with God and urged David to do the same. She resisted the temptation to put everything on God and wait for Him to resolve the situation.

When someone doesn't take responsibility for their behavior but just falls on their face and puts everything on God, that is called *super spiritual passivity*. It looks like they are being more *(super) spiritual* than people around them because they are praying and waiting on God. But when there are things they should be doing, this cloak of pious behavior hides their *passivity*.

In Abigail's situation, there was a wrong that needed to be corrected quickly. If she did not do her part to correct the wrong, all the males in her family would probably be dead.

But if she had sprung into action in her own cunning apart from God, that would also be wrong. Abigail trusted in God's promises and reminded David to do the same.

Abigail's humility is stunning. How many rich women, with 5 personal servants, could stay so humble? Her reaction to David's wedding proposal was to say she would wash David's servant's feet! What was the secret to her humility? She understood God is the One who provides. Anything she had that was good, was made possible by Him. She was grateful, not proud.

Giving up vengeance is sometimes difficult. We want justice and consequences now. When evil actions are returned for our good actions, we are faced with a choice. We either choose to trust God to handle justice in His time, or we mete out our own version of justice. The only problem handing out our version of vengeance is God says don't do that. He says vengeance is His.

That was Abigail's message to David. Don't avenge yourself. That is God's job. Fortunately, David listened to her. It helped that Abigail was righting Nabal's wrong. But, David could have taken the food and insisted Nabal still needed to pay for his behavior. It is a good thing he was humble enough to back off his vigilante justice. God took care of Nabal and Abigail was happy to marry David, a man she continued to respect.

Have you ever tried to counsel someone who is really angry? Or, have YOU ever been really angry and had someone try to counsel you? Humble respect, with talk of righting the wrong, works better than just lecturing. David had no doubt Abigail understood the wrong he was responding to. She admitted the grievous wrong and then made an effort to correct it. If she just came empty handed, lecturing David about allowing God to handle vengeance, there is a chance that would not have been enough to calm his rage. David felt understood and respected which helped him act respectfully. When you are angry, it helps to be understood and respected. Remember this, the next time you are counseling someone who is very angry.

Abigail did something else right. She had good instincts about timing. She hurried to meet David and right the wrong. But, she delayed talking with Nabal. She did not try and reason with him, she just sprung into action. He was an arrogant, evil fool. He would have stopped her. When she got back from saving his life, she did not try and tell him what a fool he had been. He was drunk. She was wise enough to not try to reason with a drunk. Many a woman would not have the maturity to wait. They would need to tell Nabal right away that they had saved him and his household from disaster.

Timing matters. He did not argue the next morning through the blur of his choices. Things tend to work out, in the long run, for those who obey, and trust God to handle vengeance.

What God Is Like

- *1. God is a "Hands-On" parent.* He wants us to trust Him to avenge for us when we have been wronged. He cares when we are treated unjustly. He protects His children as they fight His battles.

- *2. God is not impulsive.* He waited 10 days before taking Nabal's life.

- *3. God shares His riches with the just and the unjust.* He wants us to share too.

*"God wants us
to give Him our best
so that He can
give us His best."*

the Authors

Passage 7:
Ruth ~ Loyal Love

The stories of Ruth and her suitor Boaz are intermingled in this passage and in the next passage. As you *Flicker* this passage focus on what you see and learn about Ruth as she interacts with each person.

If you look at each event in this passage from several points of view you will get additional *Lessons*. For example, when when Ruth says she will stay with Naomi even though her husband has died look for *Lessons* from the point of view of Naomi, then switch and look at the same event from Ruth's point of view. What was she feeling, what do you think caused her to choose the foreign mother-in-law, how do you think she addressed the insecurities and risks this imposed on Ruth?

There is a strong theme of vulnerability and risk in Ruth's life. How did she address those feelings? Do you think she ignored them? If not, how do you think she address them?

Try not to view the scene in the threshing floor when she sleeps at the feet of Boaz like it is similar to a sex scene in a current day romantic drama. Up to that point in the story Boaz had made all the overtures about his interest in her. This was a tangible display of her interest in him. Also notice that she was not lying down beside him or with him. She lay at his feet. She was making herself vulnerable to him because she trusted him and her action would communicate that very clearly.

Ruth 1:1 Now it came about in the days when the judges governed, that there was a famine in the land. And a certain man of Bethlehem in Judah went to sojourn in the land of Moab with his wife and his two sons.

Ruth 1:2 The name of the man [was] Elimelech, and the name of his wife, Naomi; and the names of his two sons [were] Mahlon and Chilion, Ephrathites of Bethlehem in Judah. Now they entered the land of Moab and remained there.

Ruth 1:3 Then Elimelech, Naomi's husband, died; and she was left with her two sons.

Ruth 1:4 They took for themselves Moabite women [as] wives; the name of the one was Orpah and the name of the other Ruth. And they lived there about ten years.

Ruth 1:5 Then both Mahlon and Chilion also died, and the woman was bereft of her two children and her husband.

Ruth 1:6 Then she arose with her daughters-in-law that she might return from the land of Moab, for she had heard in the land of Moab that the LORD had visited His people in giving them food.

Ruth 1:7 So she departed from the place where she was, and her two daughters-in-law with her; and they went on the way to return to the land of Judah.

Ruth 1:8 And Naomi said to her two daughters-in-law, "Go, return each of you to her mother's house. May the LORD deal kindly with you as you have dealt with the dead and with me.

Ruth 1:9 "May the LORD grant that you may find rest, each in the house of her husband." Then she kissed them, and they lifted up their voices and wept.

Ruth 1:10 And they said to her, "[No,] but we will surely return with you to your people."

Ruth 1:11 But Naomi said, "Return, my daughters. Why should you go with me? Have I yet sons in my womb, that they may be your husbands?

Ruth 1:12 "Return, my daughters! Go, for I am too old to have a husband. If I said I have hope, if I should even have a husband tonight and also bear sons,

Ruth 1:13 would you therefore wait until they were grown? Would you therefore refrain from marrying? No, my daughters; for it is harder for me than for you, for the hand of the LORD has gone forth against me."

Ruth 1:14 And they lifted up their voices and wept again; and Orpah kissed her mother-in-law, but Ruth clung to her.

Ruth 1:15 Then she said, "Behold, your sister-in-law has gone back to her people and her gods; return after your sister-in-law."

Ruth 1:16 But Ruth said, "Do not urge me to leave you [or] turn back from following you; for where you go, I will go, and where you lodge, I will lodge. Your people [shall be] my people, and your God, my God.

Ruth 1:17 "Where you die, I will die, and there I will be buried. Thus may the LORD do to me, and worse, if [anything but] death parts you and me."

Ruth 1:18 When she saw that she was determined to go with her, she said no more to her.

Ruth 1:19 So they both went until they came to Bethlehem. And when they had come to Bethlehem, all the city was stirred because of them, and the women said, "Is this Naomi?"

Ruth 1:20 She said to them, "Do not call me Naomi; call me Mara, for the Almighty has dealt very bitterly with me.

Ruth 1:21 "I went out full, but the LORD has brought me back empty. Why do you call me Naomi, since the LORD has witnessed against me and the Almighty has afflicted me?"

Ruth 1:22 So Naomi returned, and with her Ruth the Moabitess, her daughter-in-law, who returned from the land of Moab. And they came to Bethlehem at the beginning of barley harvest.

Ruth 2:1 Now Naomi had a kinsman of her husband, a man of great wealth, of the family of Elimelech, whose name was Boaz.

Ruth 2:2 And Ruth the Moabitess said to Naomi, "Please let me go to the field and glean among the ears of grain after one in whose sight I may find favor." And she said to her, "Go, my daughter."

Ruth 2:3 So she departed and went and gleaned in the field after the reapers; and she happened to come to the portion of the field belonging to Boaz, who was of the family of Elimelech.

Ruth 2:4 Now behold, Boaz came from Bethlehem and said to the reapers, "May the LORD be with you." And they said to him, "May the LORD bless you."

Ruth 2:5 Then Boaz said to his servant who was in charge of the reapers, "Whose young woman is this?"

Ruth 2:6 The servant in charge of the reapers replied, "She is the young Moabite woman who returned with Naomi from the land of Moab.

Ruth 2:7 "And she said, 'Please let me glean and gather after the reapers among the sheaves.' Thus she came and has remained from the morning until now; she has been sitting in the house for a little while."

Ruth 2:8 Then Boaz said to Ruth, "Listen carefully, my daughter. Do not go to glean in another field; furthermore, do not go on from this one, but stay here with my maids.

Ruth 2:9 "Let your eyes be on the field which they reap, and go after them. Indeed, I have commanded the servants not to touch you. When you are thirsty, go to the water jars and drink from what the servants draw."

Ruth 2:10 Then she fell on her face, bowing to the ground and said to him, "Why have I found favor in your sight that you should take notice of me, since I am a foreigner?"

Ruth 2:11 Boaz replied to her, "All that you have done for your mother-in-law after the death of your husband has been fully reported to me, and how you left your father and your mother and the land of your birth, and came to a people that you did not previously know.

Ruth 2:12 "May the LORD reward your work, and your wages be full from the LORD, the God of Israel, under whose wings you have come to seek refuge."

Ruth 2:13 Then she said, "I have found favor in your sight, my lord, for you have comforted me and indeed have spoken kindly to your maidservant, though I am not like one of your maidservants."

Ruth 2:14 At mealtime Boaz said to her, "Come here, that you may eat of the bread and dip your piece of bread in the vinegar." So she sat beside the reapers; and he served her roasted grain, and she ate and was satisfied and had some left.

Ruth 2:15 When she rose to glean, Boaz commanded his servants, saying, "Let her glean even among the sheaves, and do not insult her.

Ruth 2:16 "Also you shall purposely pull out for her [some grain] from the bundles and leave [it] that she may glean, and do not rebuke her."

Ruth 2:17 So she gleaned in the field until evening. Then she beat out what she had gleaned, and it was about an ephah of barley.

Ruth 2:18 She took [it] up and went into the city, and her mother-in-law saw what she had gleaned. She also took [it] out and gave Naomi what she had left after she was satisfied.

Ruth 2:19 Her mother-in-law then said to her, "Where did you glean today and where did you work? May he who took notice of you be blessed." So she told her mother-in-law with whom she had worked and said, "The name of the man with whom I worked today is Boaz."

Ruth 2:20 Naomi said to her daughter-in-law, "May he be blessed of the LORD who has not withdrawn his kindness to the living and to the dead." Again Naomi said to her, "The man is our relative, he is one of our closest relatives."

Ruth 2:21 Then Ruth the Moabitess said, "Furthermore, he said to me, 'You should stay close to my servants until they have finished all my harvest.'"

Ruth 2:22 Naomi said to Ruth her daughter-in-law, "It is good, my daughter, that you go out with his maids, so that [others] do not fall upon you in another field."

Ruth 2:23 So she stayed close by the maids of Boaz in order to glean until the end of the barley harvest and the wheat harvest. And she lived with her mother-in-law.

Passage 7—Ruth 1:1-3:18

Ruth 3:1 Then Naomi her mother-in-law said to her, "My daughter, shall I not seek security for you, that it may be well with you?

Ruth 3:2 "Now is not Boaz our kinsman, with whose maids you were? Behold, he winnows barley at the threshing floor tonight.

Ruth 3:3 "Wash yourself therefore, and anoint yourself and put on your [best] clothes, and go down to the threshing floor; [but] do not make yourself known to the man until he has finished eating and drinking.

Ruth 3:4 "It shall be when he lies down, that you shall notice the place where he lies, and you shall go and uncover his feet and lie down; then he will tell you what you shall do."

Ruth 3:5 She said to her, "All that you say I will do."

Ruth 3:6 So she went down to the threshing floor and did according to all that her mother-in-law had commanded her.

Ruth 3:7 When Boaz had eaten and drunk and his heart was merry, he went to lie down at the end of the heap of grain; and she came secretly, and uncovered his feet and lay down.

Ruth 3:8 It happened in the middle of the night that the man was startled and bent forward; and behold, a woman was lying at his feet.

Ruth 3:9 He said, "Who are you?" And she answered, "I am Ruth your maid. So spread your covering over your maid, for you are a close relative."

Ruth 3:10 Then he said, "May you be blessed of the LORD, my daughter. You have shown your last kindness to be better than the first by not going after young men, whether poor or rich.

Ruth 3:11 "Now, my daughter, do not fear. I will do for you whatever you ask, for all my people in the city know that you are a woman of excellence.

Ruth 3:12 "Now it is true I am a close relative; however, there is a relative closer than I.

Ruth 3:13 *"Remain this night, and when morning comes, if he will redeem you, good; let him redeem you. But if he does not wish to redeem you, then I will redeem you, as the LORD lives. Lie down until morning."*

Ruth 3:14 *So she lay at his feet until morning and rose before one could recognize another; and he said, "Let it not be known that the woman came to the threshing floor."*

Ruth 3:15 *Again he said, "Give me the cloak that is on you and hold it." So she held it, and he measured six [measures] of barley and laid [it] on her. Then she went into the city.*

Ruth 3:16 *When she came to her mother-in-law, she said, "How did it go, my daughter?" And she told her all that the man had done for her.*

Ruth 3:17 *She said, "These six [measures] of barley he gave to me, for he said, 'Do not go to your mother-in-law empty-handed.'"*

Ruth 3:18 *Then she said, "Wait, my daughter, until you know how the matter turns out; for the man will not rest until he has settled it today." (NASB1995)*

FLCR **FACTS**

Ruth said she would follow Naomi.

God can use unlikely people to provide for us.

FLCR CHALLENGES

Do I believe that God can provide for me through the weak and the poor?

FLCR RESPONSES

Commentary

God can use unlikely people to provide for us. We tend to expect someone of means to be the provider—a boss type. Someone we look up to. We don't expect a poor person to come to our rescue. But, God used the poor widow Ruth to provide for Naomi. The fact that God used a widowed woman in that culture (who was also a foreigner) to provide security for Naomi is a testimony to God. He blesses and enables those who take shelter in Him. If we think He can only use rich people to provide for us then we have a small view of God.

It is a good thing that Ruth did not rule out her own ability to help. The normal thing for someone in her situation would have been to go home to the safety of her parent's house. She could have justified leaving because she had no money and no job. But she wanted to help Naomi because she loved her. She committed herself to Naomi, to her people, and to her God and that was enough to place her under God's protection. Her work ethic, humility and excellent character gave God much to bless. God wants us to give Him our best (no matter how small) so that He can give us His best. We have a small view of God when we think we can help someone only if we have extra resources.

Have you noticed that God allows things to look bleak at times? This tests our view of Him and ourselves. Do we see Him as our security? Do we place ourselves under His care? Are we creative in finding work options? Do we humbly consider the suggestions of our elders? Do we really believe that if we take shelter in God and do our part to help others and ourselves, He will provide?

God honors those who look to Him and work with humble excellence.

What God Is Like

- *1. God is powerful.* He can use people who have no resources or power (Ruth) to provide for someone in need (Naomi). He does not want us to discount what He can do through us when we have little to offer.

- *2. God is not intimidated by our large problems.* He does not prevent our problems from getting big. He allows our problems to get severe sometimes so that we take shelter in Him and reach out to help each other.

Passage 8:
Boaz ~ Compassionate Protector

When you are trusting in God is there any call to use shrewd business tactics? Does God prefer that you avoid the use of rhetoric and posturing when negotiating so the final conclusion is the result of His will alone?

Although there are some times that God does take absolute control of a situation, His normal preference is for us to do everything we can do while trusting and resolved that God will guide and enable the direction He wants us to take.

Boaz was smitten by Ruth and wanted to secure her hand but please notice that he did not dispassionately lay out all the facts before the one that had the first option for her hand and passively wait for the fellow's decision. Boaz made his best case as passionately and shrewdly as he could then rested in God's superintending guidance.

As you *Flicker* his negotiation for Ruth notice how beautifully Boaz skill, God's sovereignty, and Boaz depth of character work together to cause the final result.

Ruth 4:1 Now Boaz went up to the gate and sat down there, and behold, the close relative of whom Boaz spoke was passing by, so he said, "Turn aside, friend, sit down here." And he turned aside and sat down.

Ruth 4:2 He took ten men of the elders of the city and said, "Sit down here." So they sat down.

Ruth 4:3 Then he said to the closest relative, "Naomi, who has come back from the land of Moab, has to sell the piece of land which belonged to our brother Elimelech.

Ruth 4:4 "So I thought to inform you, saying, 'Buy [it] before those who are sitting [here,] and before the elders of my people. If you will redeem [it,] redeem [it;] but if not, tell me that I may know; for there is no one but you to redeem [it,] and I am after you.'" And he said, "I will redeem [it.]"

Ruth 4:5 Then Boaz said, "On the day you buy the field from the hand of Naomi, you must also acquire Ruth the Moabitess, the widow of the deceased, in order to raise up the name of the deceased on his inheritance."

Ruth 4:6 The closest relative said, "I cannot redeem [it] for myself, because I would jeopardize my own inheritance. Redeem [it] for yourself; you [may have] my right of redemption, for I cannot redeem [it.]"

Ruth 4:7 Now this was [the custom] in former times in Israel concerning the redemption and the exchange [of land] to confirm any matter: a man removed his sandal and gave it to another; and this was the [manner of] attestation in Israel.

Ruth 4:8 So the closest relative said to Boaz, "Buy [it] for yourself." And he removed his sandal.

Ruth 4:9 Then Boaz said to the elders and all the people, "You are witnesses today that I have bought from the hand of Naomi all that belonged to Elimelech and all that belonged to Chilion and Mahlon.

Ruth 4:10 "Moreover, I have acquired Ruth the Moabitess, the widow of Mahlon, to be my wife in order to raise up the name of the deceased on his inheritance, so that the name of the deceased will not be cut off from his brothers or from the court of his [birth] place; you are witnesses today."

Ruth 4:11 All the people who were in the court, and the elders, said, "[We are] witnesses. May the LORD make the woman who is coming into your home like Rachel and Leah, both of whom built the house of Israel; and may you achieve wealth in Ephrathah and become famous in Bethlehem.

Ruth 4:12 "Moreover, may your house be like the house of Perez whom Tamar bore to Judah, through the offspring which the LORD will give you by this young woman."

Ruth 4:13 So Boaz took Ruth, and she became his wife, and he went in to her. And the LORD enabled her to conceive, and she gave birth to a son.

Ruth 4:14 Then the women said to Naomi, "Blessed is the LORD who has not left you without a redeemer today, and may his name become famous in Israel.

Ruth 4:15 "May he also be to you a restorer of life and a sustainer of your old age; for your daughter-in-law, who loves you and is better to you than seven sons, has given birth to him."

Ruth 4:16 Then Naomi took the child and laid him in her lap, and became his nurse.

Ruth 4:17 The neighbor women gave him a name, saying, "A son has been born to Naomi!" So they named him Obed. He is the father of Jesse, the father of David.

Ruth 4:18 Now these are the generations of Perez: to Perez was born Hezron,

Ruth 4:19 and to Hezron was born Ram, and to Ram, Amminadab,

Ruth 4:20 and to Amminadab was born Nahshon, and to Nahshon, Salmon,

Ruth 4:21 and to Salmon was born Boaz, and to Boaz, Obed,

Ruth 4:22 and to Obed was born Jesse, and to Jesse, David. (NASB1995)

FLCR FACTS

Naomi's husband was related to Boaz and Boaz was very wealthy.

God likes when we take care of needy widows.

FLCR CHALLENGES

Am I willing to respond to a widow in need?

FLCR RESPONSES

Commentary

God uses people to meet needs. Boaz asked the Lord to reward Ruth's work and to bless her, but God moved him to deliver God's blessing. Just think what Boaz would have missed if he was too busy to notice the extra face among his reapers? He probably wouldn't be in the blood line of Christ, or mentioned in the Bible, or married to Ruth, or the father of her son.

His care for a lowly widow changed his life immeasurably. Boaz could have ignored Ruth, the widow, because he had more "important" things to do. But instead he took an interest in her and protected and shared with her. He was willing to put himself out for Ruth because she had an excellent reputation and worked hard. In the same way, Ruth could have gone home to her parents, but she chose to stay because she loved her mother-in-law. God likes it when we take care of needy widows.

Just like Boaz life was dramatically changed by his kindness to Ruth, Ruth's life was dramatically changed by her kindness to her widowed mother-in-law. Ruth had excellent character. She was also a widow, but she was not a complainer. She was not a victim. She was a hard working, humble, thankful, person. She did not abandon her widowed mother-in-law when things got tough. She bravely went out to work to make a difference.

Her character and reputation moved Boaz to help and protect her. She inspired respect by selflessly giving to a mother-in-law in need. God noticed both Boaz and Ruth's behavior and He made them famous to this day. Boaz probably thought he was successful because of his thriving business. God probably thinks Boaz was successful because of his kind, generous behavior as a boss and human being. He greeted his workers with a blessing. He watched out for their welfare. He made sure they were well-fed and had a place to rest. He taught them to be kind. He was discreet and faithful. Ruth was grateful to be treated like one of his servants.

Boaz seems a bit like God. God blesses us, He shares with us, He watches out for our welfare, He meets our needs, and He teaches us to be kind. We should be grateful to be one of His servants. I would hate to get to heaven and look back over my life and see missed opportunities to be kind to a noble person in need that would have dramatically changed the course of both of our lives. It would be doubly hard to see that God gave me the chance first, but had to find someone else to respond to their need.

May we not just pray for the poor, may we recognize when we are also the answer to those prayers.

What God Is Like

- *1. God cares about the poor.* He does not prevent us from falling into great need, but He urges His children who do have resources to share with those in need. God loves to share and be generous and He wants us to be like Him. If He did not allow need, we would not learn to share.

- *2. God is impressed by little acts of kindness.* We are harder to impress. We want big, impressive acts. God is humbler than us.

*"Ruth did not
assume the role
of a victim."*

the Authors

Appendix:
Answers

More answers are given below than you are expected to find when you study the passages. Most people find four to six *Facts*, one or two *Lessons*, one or two *Challenges*, and one *Response* when they study a passage. Extra answers are given here to help you better recognize *Facts*, *Lessons*, *Challenges*, and *Responses*.

1—Able ~ Murdered For His Faith   13
(Genesis 4:1-17, Hebrews 11:4)

Facts

- Adam had relations with his wife Eve
- She gave birth to Cain
- Eve said "I have gotten a man from the LORD"
- She gave birth to his brother Abel
- Abel tended flocks
- Cain tilled the ground
- Cain brought an offering of produce to the Lord
- Abel brought the fattest firstborns of his flock
- The LORD was pleased with Abel and his offering
- The LORD was not pleased with Cain and his offering
- Cain become very angry and his countenance fell
- The LORD asked Cain...
- ...Why are you angry?
- ...Why has your countenance fallen?
- ...If you do well won't you be accepted?
- ...If you don't do well sin waits at the door desiring you
- ...But you must master it
- While they were in the field Cain killed Abel
- The LORD asked Cain...
- ...Where is Abel your brother?
- Cain said...
- ...I do not know. Am I my brother's keeper?
- God said...
- ...What have you done?
- ...The voice of your brother's blood is crying to Me from the ground
- ...Now you are cursed from the ground which has received your brother's blood from your hand

- ...When you cultivate the ground it will no longer yield its best to you
- ...You will be a homeless wanderer on the earth
- Cain said to the LORD...
- ...My punishment is too much to bear
- ...You have driven me from the face of the ground and from Your face
- ...I will be a homeless wanderer on the earth
- ...Whoever finds me will kill me
- The LORD said to him...
- ...Whoever kills you will have sevenfold vengeance taken on him
- The LORD gave Cain a sign so no one would kill him
- Cain left the presence of the LORD and settled in the land of Nod, east of Eden
- Cain had relations with his wife and she gave birth to Enoch
- He built a city and called it Enoch after his son.
- ...
- Abel offered his sacrifice to God by faith
- Abel's faith made his sacrifice better than Cain's
- Abel's faith made him righteous
- God testified about Abel's offering
- Even though Abel is dead, he still speaks through his faith

Lessons

- It can look like evil triumphs sometimes. God allowed Cain to overpower and kill Abel. But, looks can be deceiving. God has a bigger perspective. The story does not end with Cain prevailing against Abel. Abel has been famous for centuries because of his faith-filled offering. He is the one who triumphs. He has inspired many to follow his example of grateful giving back to God.
- It is possible to please the Lord with our behavior
- Faith in the God Who provides has always been the way to please God. Long before placing our faith in Jesus' atonement, Abel placed his faith in the God Who provided for him. It takes faith to give back to God some of the best He has provided for us.
- Abel's faith made him righteous. His offering (or works) did not make him righteous. His good offering flowed from his faith and gratitude for the God Who provides.
- As a parent it is possible to raise one righteous child and one evil child. Parents don't control all the factors. Parents are in charge of the home environment, but genetics cause personality predispositions and the child's personal choices influence outcome.
- We need to be aware that sin is waiting for an opportunity to overtake us. We can master sin by being vigilant to choose to do what is right, even after we have done wrong.

Challenges

- Do I believe that God is just and will triumph in the end?
- Do I believe that God can work all things together for good for me, even if it looks like evil is winning?
- Am I pleasing God with my faith in Him as the one Who provides?
- Am I giving Him back a portion of the best He has provided for me?
- Do I realize it is my faith that makes me righteous and not my works?

- Do my good works flow from my faith and gratitude for God Who provides for me?
- Am I taking too much credit if my child turns out good?
- Am I taking too much credit if my child turns out poorly?
- Do I realize sin is waiting for an opportunity to overtake me?
- Am I being vigilant to choose to do what is right?
- Am I vigilant to choose to do right even after I have done wrong?

Responses

- Lord, please help me to know You so that I understand what You want and my faith and obedience flow out of my gratitude and love for Who You are.

2—Sarah ~ One Who Had Wavering Faith   23
(Genesis 16:1-6; 18:1,10-15; Hebrews 11:11)

Facts

- Sarai, Abram's wife, was childless with Abram.
- She had an Egyptian maid named Hagar.
- She told Abram to have a child with Hagar because the Lord had prevented her from conceiving.
- Abram listened to Sarai.
- After living in Canaan for ten years, Sarai gave Abram Hagar to be his wife.
- After Hagar conceived she despised Sarai.
- Sarai blamed Abram and asked the Lord to judge who was to blame.
- Abram told Sarai to exercise her authority over Hagar.
- Sarai started to treat her harshly.
- Hagar fled.
- The Lord appeared to Abram in the heat of the day while he sat by the oaks of Mamre.
- The Lord told Abram He would return next year and Sarai would have a son.
- Sarai was listening at the tent door.
- Abraham and Sarai were old.
- Sarai was past childbearing age.
- Sarai laughed to herself thinking how unlikely this was.
- The Lord asked Abraham why Sarai laughed saying "Will I really have a child when I am old?"
- The Lord said "Is anything too difficult for the Lord?"
- He told them at the appointed time next year I will come and Sarai will have a son.
- Sarai denied laughing because she was afraid.
- The Lord said "No, you did laugh."
- ...
- Sarah's faith enabled her to conceive.

- She was beyond the proper time of life for conception.
- Sarah considered Him faithful who had promised.

Lessons

- The Lord prevents and enables conception for His reasons. The timing of Sarai's conception was "appointed."
- We might have to wait for years to see God fulfill His promises to us.
- If we give up on God and take matters into our own hands we can make things worse.
- God did not prevent Hagar from conceiving to control the consequences of Sarai and Abram's sin. My sin can hurt others.
- Having authority over someone does not mean we can treat them badly.
- Nothing is too difficult for the Lord. He wants us to ponder this, and then believe it.
- When we have the sin of unbelief we should just admit it and not lie. God knows the truth. He wants us to respect Him enough to be honest with Him.
- God keeps His promises even when we sin.
- When we abuse our power and cause someone else to sin they will resent us.
- In spite of your stumbling God can use your faith.

Challenges

- Do I believe that God prevents and enables conception?
- Do I trust His reasons when He prevents and enables conception?
- Do I believe He "appoints" His children's birthdays?
- Am I willing to wait for years, trusting God to fulfill some of His promises to me?
- While I wait, will I resist the temptation to take matters into my own hands?
- Do I see waiting may be painful, but taking matters into my own hands can make things worse?
- Do I see that God won't prevent sin if I choose to act out? (He did not keep Hagar from conceiving to hide Sarai and Abram's sin).
- Do I realize my sin can hurt others, or do I think it only affects me?
- Do I trust God to do the right thing? (Even if I have to wait years to see Him fulfill a promise)?
- Am I willing to accept responsibility for my sin and not shift the blame to someone else?
- When I have authority, do I use it well?
- Am I willing to ponder His question "Is anything too difficult for the Lord?" and believe it? Do I live like I believe it?
- When I doubt God's Word, am I willing to confess this to God because He already knows the truth?
- Am I honest with God?
- Do I believe God will keep His promises even when I sin, or do I think my behavior controls Him?
- Am I willing to take responsibility and ask forgiveness when I abuse my power as a parent, employer or elder?

- Do I see how people resent being abused when they don't have the power to decide for themselves?
- Do I believe God focuses on my faith even when I have stumbled?

Responses

- Father, forgive me when I take matters into my own hand and don't wait and trust You to do what you've promised.
- Thank you for keeping Your promises and doing it in Your time. You know best.

3—Rahab ~ An Unlikely Ally 33
(Joshua 2:1-21; Hebrews 11:31)

Facts

- Joshua sent two spies to view Jericho and the rest of the land.
- The two spies came to stay at Rahab's house.
- Rahab was a harlot.
- The King of Jericho heard about the spies from Israel.
- The King of Jericho asked Rahab to give him the spies.
- Rahab hid the spies on her roof under stalks of flax.
- She lied saying she did not know where they were from.
- She lied saying they left at night and she did not know where they went.
- She told them they could catch them if they chased after them.
- They pursued them as she suggested.
- Rahab came to the roof.
- She said she knew the Lord had given them the land.
- She said the terror of Israel was on them because...
- ...They had heard how God dried up the water of the Red Sea for them when they left Egypt
- ...They saw the annihilation of the two Amorite Kings, Sihon and Og
- Because of this she proclaimed the LORD your God is the God in heaven above and on earth beneath.
- Rahab asked the spies to swear to her by the LORD that they would save her and her family since she was kind to them.
- The spies said if she would keep them a secret they would faithfully save them.
- Rahab let them climb down a rope through the window to escape.
- Rahab told them to go to the hill country and hide for 3 days until the pursuers gave up and returned.
- The spies said they would be free of their oath if Rahab did not have a cord of scarlet in the window and her whole family stayed in her house.
- If any of her family went outside and got killed, they were free of their oath.
- If she told their secret, they were free of their oath.
- Rahab agreed.
- The spies departed.

- Rahab tied the scarlet cord in the window.

- ...

- Rahab did not perish because of her faith in God.

- She welcomed the spies in peace.

- The other people in Jericho were called "the disobedient."

Lessons

- God uses unlikely people for His purposes. Rahab had morality issues, but she had new faith in the God of Israel as the true God in heaven and on earth. God used her for His purposes.

- God uses us as we are. Rahab lied to protect the spies. God seemed to overlook this because of her new faith and fear of Him, and because she was cooperating with His purposes. We don't have to be perfect to be used by God. Instead of focusing on ourselves, it is better to focus on God. The longer we walk with God, the less morality issues we will have, but God can use us as we are.

- It takes courage to follow God sometimes. Rahab had to decide whom she feared more: the King of Jericho, or the God of Israel. It took courage for her to trust God, and betray the King of Jericho. It took courage for the spies to go into enemy territory trusting God to see them through.

Challenges

- Do I only listen to people who fit my profile of who God should use?

- Do I think God could use me for His purposes?

- Is my faith in the God of the Bible?

- Do I fear the God of the Bible?

- Do I think I need to get sinless before God will use me?

- Is my focus on myself, or on God?

- Am I cooperating with God's purpose?

- Am I improving the longer I walk with God?

- Am I willing to choose God over everything else, even if I am afraid?

- Do I believe God will see me through whatever He asks me to do?

Responses

- Father, forgive me when I focus too much on myself and my sins and not enough on You and Your purposes.

- Thank You for using the faith of a harlot. Help me to focus on You and Your power like she did.

4—Hannah ~ God Uses The Humble   43
(1 Samuel 1:1-2:12)

Facts

- A man from Ephraim named Elkanah, son of Jeroham had two wives.

- One was Hannah and the other was Peninnah.

- Peninnah had children.

- Hannah had no children.

- Elkanah went from his city each year to worship and sacrifice to the LORD of armies in Shiloh.

- Eli's two sons Hophni and Phinehas were priests to the LORD there.

- When Elkanah sacrificed he would give portions to his wife Peninnah and her sons and daughters.
- But he gave Hannah a double portion because he loved her, but God had closed her womb.
- Her rival would provoke her bitterly to irritate her because God had closed her womb.
- Year after year when they went to the house of the LORD she provoked her.
- Hannah wept and would not eat.
- Elkanah asked her why she wept and would not eat.
- He asked her wasn't he better to her than 10 sons.
- Hannah got up after eating and drinking.
- Eli the priest was sitting by the doorpost of the temple.
- Hannah prayed to the LORD and wept bitterly.
- She made a vow.
- She prayed to the "LORD of armies."
- She said if God would see her affliction as His bond-servant and give her a son, then she would give him to God all the days of his life and a razor would never be used on his head.
- Eli watched her mouth.
- She was speaking in her heart, but her lips quivered.
- Eli thought she was drunk.
- Eli said "how long will you behave drunk, get rid of your wine.
- Hannah answered "no my lord, I am a woman despairing in spirit. I have not been drinking vine or strong drink. I poured out my soul to the LORD.
- Do not think I am a worthless woman. I have spoken out of great grief.
- Eli said "go in peace; May the God of Israel grant your petition."
- Hannah said "let your bond servant find favor in your sight."
- She left, and was no longer sad.
- They got up early, worshipped and returned to their house.
- Elkanah had relations with Hannah.
- God remembered her.
- She conceived and gave birth to a son.
- She named him Samuel because "I have asked for him of the Lord."
- Elkanah went with his household to offer the yearly sacrifice and pay his vow.
- Hannah did not go until Samuel was weaned.
- She would go when he could appear before the LORD and stay there for life.
- Elkanah told her to do what she thought best, only have the LORD confirm His word.
- She stayed and nursed him until he was weaned.
- Once he was weaned she took him with her,
- With a three year old bull, half a bushel of flour and a jug of wine.
- Samuel was young.

- They slaughtered the bull and brought the boy to Eli.
- She told Eli she was the one praying to the LORD.
- She said she prayed for this boy and God answered.
- She said she dedicated him to God for his whole life.
- They worshipped the LORD there.
- ...(Chapter 2)...
- Hannah prayed and worshipped the LORD.
- Her heart exults in the LORD.
- Her mouth speaks boldly against her enemies.
- Because she rejoiced in God's salvation.
- She said there is no one holy like the LORD.
- No one like You.
- There is no rock like our God.
- We can't boast or be arrogant.
- God is a God of knowledge.
- He weighs actions.
- The bows of the mighty are shattered.
- The feeble gird on strength.
- The full become needy and the hungry cease to be hungry.
- The barren gives birth to seven.
- The one with many children languishes.
- The LORD kills and makes alive.
- He brings down to Sheol and raises up.
- He makes poor and rich.
- He brings low and exalts.
- He raises the poor and lifts the needy to sit with nobles in a seat of honor.
- The pillars of the earth are the LORD's.
- He set the world on them.
- He keeps the feet of His godly ones.
- The wicked ones are silenced in darkness.
- A man will not prevail by might.
- Those who fight the Lord will be shattered.
- The LORD judges the earth.
- He gives strength to His king.
- He exalts the horn of His anointed.
- Elkanah went home.
- The boy ministered to the LORD before Eli the priest.

Lessons

- Our desperation can be an answer to God. God was looking for a priest after His heart and soul in 2:35. Hannah was looking to conceive. Hannah's desperation answered God's desire for a devoted priest so He enabled her to conceive. Win/Win. Without desperation Hannah would not have offered God her son.

- Man cannot prevail against the Lord by might. It is better to align ourselves with God's purposes.

Challenges

- Do I realize my needs might have a purpose for God?
- Am I aligned with God's purpose or fighting it?
- Do I see that a heart for God can survive and thrive even in a corrupt environment?

Responses

- Thank You Lord for matching our desperation with Your good will.
- Please help me not waste my life being too rigid and desperate to recognize Your will.
- Thank You for being powerful enough to accomplish Your will in spite of me.
- Please help me to be part of what You are accomplishing like Hannah was part of giving You a faithful priest.

5—Samuel ~ God Uses The Sincere   55
(1 Samuel 2:12, 18-21, 34-36, 3:1-21)

Facts

- Eli's sons were worthless.
- They did not know the LORD.
- Samuel was ministering before the Lord.
- He was a boy wearing a linen apron that priests wear.
- His mother would make him a robe and bring it each year when they came to offer their yearly sacrifice.
- Eli would bless Elkanah and Hannah and ask God to bless them with more children since she dedicated Samuel to God.
- They went home.
- God blessed Hannah and she conceived.
- She gave birth to three sons and two daughters.
- Samuel grew before the Lord.
- Samuel was growing up in favor with God and men.
- Concerning your two sons, Hophni and Phinehas, they will die on the same day.
- I will raise up for Myself a faithful priest.
- He will do what is in My heart and soul.
- I will build him a permanent, enduring house.
- He will walk before My anointed forever.
- Whoever is left in your house will bow down to him for a piece of silver or bread.
- He will ask him to give him a job as a priest so he can eat some bread.
- The boy Samuel was ministering to the LORD before Eli.
- A word from God was rare then,
- Visions were infrequent.
- Eli was lying down.

- His eyesight was poor.
- The lamp of God had not gone out.
- Samuel was lying down in the temple of the LORD where the ark of God was.
- The LORD called Samuel.
- Samuel said "here I am."
- He ran to Eli and said "here I am, you called me."
- Eli said "I did not call lie down again."
- Samuel went and lay down.
- The LORD called "Samuel."
- Samuel got up and went to Eli and said "Here I am for you called me."
- Eli said "I did not call my son, lie down again."
- Samuel did not yet know the LORD,
- Nor had the word of the LORD been revealed to him.
- The LORD called Samuel a third time.
- He went to Eli and said "Here I am for you called me,."
- Eli discerned the LORD was calling the boy.
- Eli told Samuel to lie down.
- If He calls you say "Speak LORD, Your servant is listening."
- Samuel lay down in his place.
- The LORD came and stood and called again "Samuel, Samuel."
- Samuel said "Speak for Your servant is listening."
- The LORD said I am about to do a thing in Israel which will make everyone who hears both ears tingle.
- I will carry out against Eli all I have spoken concerning his house, from beginning to end.
- I have told him I am about to judge his house forever for the sin which he knew.
- His sons brought a curse on themselves.
- He did not rebuke them.
- The sin of Eli will not be atoned for by sacrifice or offering forever.
- Samuel lay down until morning.
- He opened the doors of the house of the LORD.
- He was afraid to tell the vision to Eli.
- Eli called Samuel.
- Samuel said "Here I am."
- Eli asked what is the word He spoke to you?
- Eli told him not to hide it from him.
- Eli told Samuel God would do to him and more so if he hides His words from him.
- Samuel told him everything.
- Eli said "It is the LORD, let Him do what seems good to Him."
- Samuel grew and the LORD was with him.
- God did not let any of Samuel's words fail.

- All Israel knew Samuel was confirmed as God's prophet.
- God continued to appear to Samuel at Shiloh.

Lessons

- Eli raised two wicked sons, but Samuel was not spoiled by his environment. He chose the Lord and the Lord was with him.
- God will only tolerate wicked behavior by the clergy for awhile.
- Parents are responsible for their children when they practice blatant sins against God under their care.
- God honors those who honor Him.
- God is in charge of when we die.
- We should not put our wicked children ahead of our devotion to God.
- God wants us to care about His heart.
- God was extremely generous to Samuel who served Him with loyal obedience.

Challenges

- Do I trust God to purge evil from His church?
- Do I put God first over my children?
- Do I honor God?
- Do I trust God with when I die?
- Do I care about God's heart?
- Do I see how generous God is with those who generously serve Him?
- Do I see how devotion to God takes first place over wicked children?

Responses

- Lord, help me to recognize Your voice when You want to guide me or use me.
- Thank You for using humble people.

6—Abigail ~ One Who Was Married To A Fool   65
(1 Samuel 25:2-42)

Facts

- A rich man came to Carmel on business.
- He had 3,000 sheep and 1,000 goats.
- He was shearing his sheep in Carmel.
- His name was Nabal.
- His wife's name was Abigail.
- Abigail was smart and beautiful.
- Nabal was harsh and evil in his dealings.
- He was a Calebite.
- David heard in the wilderness that Nabal was shearing his sheep.
- David sent 10 young men to Carmel to visit Nabal in his name.
- David told them to say to Nabal "have a long life, peace to you and your house and peace to all you have."
- David told them to remind Nabal his men had taken care of his

shepherds and treated them well. Nothing was stolen all the days they were in Carmel.

- The young men told Nabal to ask his workers to verify.
- Therefore let us find favor in your eyes as we have come on a festive day, please give us whatever you find at hand to your servants and your son David.
- David's young men spoke to Nabal according to these words in David's name.
- They waited.
- Nabal said "who is David, who is the son of Jesse? There are many servants today leaving their master."
- "Shall I take my bread and water and meat and give it to unknown men?."
- David's young men went back.
- They told David what he had said.
- David told them to gird on their sword which they did.
- David led 400 men while 200 stayed behind with the baggage.
- One of Nabal's shepherds told Abigail that David sent messengers to greet Nabal but he scorned them.
- He told Abigail the men were very good to us.
- They did not insult or steal from us.
- They were a wall to us day and night as we tended the sheep.
- He told Abigail to consider what to do because evil is plotted against Nabal.
- He told Abigail Nabal is so worthless no one can speak to him.
- Abigail hurried.
- She took 200 loaves of bread, 2 jugs of wine, 5 sheep already prepared and 5 measures of roasted grain and 100 clusters of raisins, 200 cakes of figs and loaded them on donkeys.
- She told the shepherd to go before her. She did not tell Nabal.
- She was riding on her donkey by the hidden part of the mountain.
- She met David and his men.
- David had said he guarded Nabal's property in the wilderness and he returned evil for good.
- David asked God to punish him greatly if he doesn't kill every male belonging to Nabal by morning.
- When Abigail saw David she hurried and dismounted from her donkey.
- She fell on her face before David and bowed to the ground.
- She fell at his feet and said "on me alone my lord, be the blame."
- She asked permission to speak that he would listen to her a maidservant.
- She asked David to ignore Nabal because he is worthless and folly is with him.
- She said she did not see the men David sent.
- She said since God has restrained you from shedding blood and avenging yourself by your own hand,
- She said let David's enemies be as Nabal.

- She asked David to accept this gift from your maidservant to be given to his young men.
- She asked David to forgive HER transgression.
- She said God would make him an enduring house because he is fighting God's battles and no evil will be found with him.
- Abigail said if anyone tries to kill David God will sling him out as from the hollow of a sling.
- And when God does all the good He spoke about you, and appoints you ruler over Israel, you will not have grief for avenging yourself. Remember your maidservant.
- David said bless be the God of Israel who sent you to meet me.
- And blessed be your discernment.
- And blessed be you for keeping me from bloodshed and avenging myself.
- If you (Abigail) had not come quickly David said no males would have survived with Nabal.
- David received her gifts.
- He told her to go to her house in peace.
- He said he had listened to her and granted her request.
- Abigail came to Nabal.
- He was holding a feast of a king in his house.
- He was merry and drunk.
- So Abigail waited until the morning to tell him.
- She told him in the morning when he was sober.
- His heart died within him like a stone.
- Ten days later God struck Nabal and he died.
- When David heard Nabal was dead he blessed the Lord for keeping him from evil and avenging Nabal's wrongdoing against him.
- Then David sent servants to propose marriage to Abigail.
- Abigail bowed and said she was a maidservant who would be a servant to wash David's servant's feet.
- Abigail quickly arose.
- She rode on a donkey with her 5 maidens who served her.
- She followed David's servants and became his wife.
- David had also taken Ahinoam of Jezreel to be his wife.
- Saul had given his daughter Michal to be David's wife, but took her from David and gave her to Palti, son of Laish.

Lessons

- Vengeance is God's. Even if evil is returned for our good, vengeance is God's. He takes care of His children.
- God wants us to be generous with those in need.
- It is wise to take action, instead of trying to reason with evil power, (Nabal) when it is in your power to right a wrong and mortal danger is imminent.
- Humble generosity can calm the desire for vengeance.
- Sometimes we need to hurry to make peace.
- Sometimes less powerful people can work to undo the imminent danger caused by powerful evil people.

- Abigail was humble and willing to accept responsibility. She did not immediately blame Nabal.

- It is wise to wait until a person is sober before reasoning with them. Timing is important when correcting someone.

- God struck Nabal ten days later. God has reasons for His timing. He is coordinating more than we see.

- It is possible to be rich, smart and beautiful and have 5 maids serving you, and still be humble, if you understand Who God is and your relationship to Him.

- Arrogant and proud people are hard to teach or reason with.

- God is kind to not answer all of our prayers. David asked Him to punish him greatly if he didn't kill all the males connected with Nabal.

- Sometimes God uses other people to speak His truth to us. He used Abigail to correct David.

- David was humble and teachable, even by a woman.

- Sometimes God avenges a wrong by ending a life.

- Nabal could have verified David's help. He probably didn't want to be generous since it says he was harsh and evil in his dealings.

- It takes faith to wait for God to do all the good He has promised. Abigail and David had faith waiting for God to fulfill His promises about David's kingship.

- A person needs to be wise to counsel someone who is angry and wanting revenge.

Challenges

- If someone returns evil for my good, am I willing to trust God to handle vengeance?

- When someone in need is kind to me am I generous in return?

- Am I willing to be brave enough to take action when there is danger or do I get passive and put it all on God?

- Do I see the power of humble generosity to calm anger for a wrongdoing?

- Do I see that timing is important for making peace?

- Do I think I need to be powerful to make peace?

- Would I be willing to accept responsibility in order to facilitate peace?

- Would I be willing to wait until Nabal was sober or would I need to tell him he was foolish right away?

- Do I trust God's timing for vengeance?

- Do I understand Who God is and my relationship with Him, or do I think money and physical gifts make me more valuable than someone poor?

- Am I teachable?

- Have I thanked God for knowing best and not answering all my prayer requests?

- Am I humble enough to listen, if God uses others to correct me?

- Am I humble and teachable?

- Am I willing to trust God if He takes someone's life?

- Do I refuse to verify because I don't want to be generous?

- Do I have faith as I wait for God to fulfill His promises to me as His child?

- Do I seek God for wisdom when I try to counsel someone who is angry?

Responses

- Father, thank You for watching out for Your children.
- Thank You for wanting justice and vengeance for us.
- May I always remember Your way is wise and will be best for me.
- Please forgive me when I am tempted to act on my own behalf.
- Thank You for being all powerful, One Who loves justice, and having love that never fails.
- Thank You that You will do the right.

7—Ruth ~ Loyal Love 77
(Ruth 1:1-3:18)

Facts

- Naomi said to her two daughters-in-law...
- ...Return to your mother's house,
- ...May the Lord deal kindly with you because you have been kind to me and your dead husbands,
- ...May the Lord give you rest in the house of a new husband.
- Naomi kissed them.
- They all wept.
- They told Naomi that they wanted to remain with her.
- Naomi told them to go home because she had no more sons for them to marry.
- They wept again.
- Orpah kissed her mother-in-law.
- Ruth clung to her.
- Naomi told Ruth to do like Orpah and return to her family and her family's gods.
- Ruth said she would follow Naomi and...
- ...lodge where she lodged,
- ...Naomi's people would become her people,
- ...Naomi's God would become her God,
- ...Where Naomi dies she would die and be buried,
- ...Ruth said the Lord should punish her if she does not keep this promise until death parts them.
- Naomi saw she was serious so she said no more.
- Ruth the Moabitess asked Naomi for permission to go and glean in the fields of those who would let her.
- Naomi told her to go.
- Boaz asked his servant in charge of the reapers who she was.
- The servant said she was a young Moabite woman who returned from Moab with Naomi.
- The servant said she asked permission to glean after the reapers among the sheaves.

- He said she worked among the reapers all day until now.
- He said she has been sitting in the house resting for a little while.
- Boaz told Ruth to listen carefully.
- He called her "daughter."
- He told her not to go to any other field to glean, but to stay with his maids.
- He commanded his servants not to touch her.
- He told her to drink from his servant's water jars if she was thirsty.
- She fell on her face, bowing to the ground.
- She wondered out loud how she had found favor in his sight since she was a foreigner.
- Boaz replied it was because of...
- ...all that she had done for her mother-in-law after the death of her own husband,
- ...her willingness to leave the familiarity of her own father and mother and land of her birth,
- Boaz asked the Lord to reward her work because she was under the God of Israel's care now.
- Ruth thanked him for his favor and comforting words even though she did not work for him.
- Naomi told Ruth she would seek security for her through Boaz their kinsman.
- Naomi knew he would harvest his barley at the threshing floor that night.
- She told Ruth to wash and anoint herself and put on her best clothes and go to the threshing floor.
- She said to wait until he is done eating and drinking.
- Notice where he lies down.
- Go and uncover his feet and lie down there.
- He will tell you what to do.
- Ruth told her she would follow all of her instructions which she did.
- Boaz asked her who she was.
- Ruth replied "I am Ruth your maid. So spread your covering over your maid for we are a close relative."
- Boaz asked the Lord to bless her. He said she was kind to seek him and not a young man, rich or poor.
- Boaz told her not to fear, he would do as she asked because she was a woman of excellence.
- Ruth became Boaz's wife.
- She conceived and gave birth to a son.
- Women blessed Naomi because the Lord did not leave her without a redeemer.
- They asked a blessing on the baby that...
- ...His name would become famous in Israel,
- ...He would restore and sustain her in her old age,
- They said her daughter-in-law's love for her was better than seven sons.

Lessons

- God can use unlikely people to provide for us. Naomi lost all of her security when her husband and sons died. Ruth had also lost her security when she became a widow. She was doubly at risk being a foreigner as well. The fact that God used a widow to provide security for Naomi is a testimony to a God who can use the meek to bless and enable those who take shelter in Him.

- A noble character finds favor with God and others. Our part is to work hard and be a person of humble excellence. This is pleasing to God and others.

- Things can look bleak, but God will help those who take shelter in Him while they do their part.

- When we help a person in need it might also help us well beyond what we imagine.

Challenges

- Do I believe God can provide for me through the weak and the poor?

- Do I believe God can provide through me for someone in need when I'm in need myself?

- Is my security in God Who can use whomever He chooses?

- Am I willing to take shelter in God?

- Am I willing to do my part by working hard, with humility and perseverance?

- Do I believe that doing my part will find favor with God and others?

- Do I believe that even though things can look bleak, if I take shelter in God and do my part, He will provide for me?

- When I have resources, am I willing to help another person in need, like Boaz?

- When I don't have resources am I willing to be creative so that I can help another person in need?

- Do I realize helping someone else will help me as well? Sometimes more than I imagine?

Responses

- Thank You Lord that You are not limited by our weakness.

- Thank You that You can use anyone for Your purposes.

- You can even use me.

- Please help me live moment by moment under the reality of Your care.

- Thank You Lord.

8—Boaz ~ Compassionate Protector   91
(Ruth 4:1-22)

Facts

- Naomi's husband was related to Boaz and Boaz was very wealthy.

- Ruth asked Naomi for permission to glean grain behind whoever would let her.

- Naomi said to go.

- Ruth went and gleaned after the reapers.

- She came to Boaz's field.

- Boaz came from Bethlehem and greeted his reapers with a blessing "May the Lord be with you."
- The reapers blessed him back "May the Lord bless you."
- Boaz asked his head reaper who Ruth was.
- The head reaper said she was the young Moabite who returned with Naomi from Moab.
- He told Boaz...
- ...she had asked for permission to glean after the reapers,
- ...she had worked since morning until now,
- ...she has been sitting in the house for a short time.
- Boaz said to Ruth...
- ...Listen carefully my daughter,
- ...Do not glean in another field,
- ...Stay here with my maids,
- ...I have commanded the servants not to touch you,
- ...If you are thirsty, drink from the servants jars.
- Ruth fell on her face, bowing.
- Ruth asked why she had found favor with Boaz since she was a foreigner.
- Boaz said he had heard how she had left her homeland and family in order to help her mother-in-law after her husband's death.
- Boaz asked the Lord to reward her work.
- Ruth told Boaz he had comforted her and treated her like she was one of his servants even though she was not.
- At mealtime Boaz allowed her to eat roasted grain with the reapers until she was satisfied and still had some left.
- When Ruth went to glean, Boaz commanded his servants to allow her to glean among the sheaves and not insult her.
- Boaz told them to purposely pull out grain from the bundles and leave it for her.
- He told them not to rebuke her.
- Naomi told Ruth that Boaz, their kinsman, would be at the threshing floor that night.
- When Boaz had finished eating and drinking and he was happy, he laid down by the grain.
- Ruth came in secretly and uncovered his feet and lay down.
- In the middle of the night Boaz was startled and saw her at his feet.
- He asked "who are you?"
- She answered "I am Ruth your maid. So spread your covering over your maid, for you are a close relative."
- Boaz asked the Lord to bless her.
- He said her last kindness was better than her first because she did not go after a young man, either poor or rich.
- He told her not to fear.
- He said he would do what she asked because everyone knew she was a woman of excellence.
- He said even though he was a close relative there was one closer.

Appendix—Answers

- He told her to remain until morning.
- If the relative redeems her, fine.
- If he does not redeem her Boaz said he would.
- He told her to lie down until morning.
- She rose early while it was still dark so no one would recognize her.
- Boaz thought it best that no one know a woman came to the threshing floor.
- He measured 60 pounds of barley into her cloak and laid it on her.
- She went into town.
- Her mother-in-law asked how it went.
- She told her all Boaz had done for her.
- She told her how Boaz gave her 60 pounds (six measures) of barley so she would not go to Naomi empty-handed.
- Boaz went to the gate and sat down until he saw the close relative.
- He asked him to sit down.
- He took 10 elders of the city and asked them to sit down.
- He said Naomi needs to sell a piece of land belonging to our brother Elimelech.
- He told him to redeem it if he wants to, and if not, he would redeem it.
- The relative said he would redeem it.
- Boaz said he would also acquire Ruth in the deal.
- The relative said he could not take on Ruth and told Boaz to redeem.
- The relative told Boaz to buy it himself.
- Boaz told the elders and people they were witnesses that today he bought from Naomi all that belonged to Elimelech and his sons including Ruth.
- He promised to raise up the name of the deceased.
- Boaz took Ruth as his wife.
- God enabled her to conceive.
- She gave birth to a son.

Lessons

- God likes when we take care of needy widows. Ruth could have gone home to her parents, but she chose to stay and help her needy, widowed, mother-in-law. Boaz could have ignored widowed Ruth, because he was the "important boss," but he took an interest in her and protected and shared with her. Boaz was willing to put himself out to protect and share with Ruth because she had an excellent reputation and worked hard.
- Boaz asked the Lord to bless and reward Ruth's work, but the Lord used him to bless and reward her.
- God wants us to be shrewd in business. Boaz was careful, direct and shrewd in business. He gathered witnesses and went by the book to redeem Ruth. Christians need to follow his example and be careful, direct and shrewd in their business dealings.
- Boaz might have promised to raise up descendants for Mahlon and his father Elimelech, but God was the one who enabled Ruth to conceive.

Challenges

- Am I willing to respond to a widow in need?
- Am I like Boaz, aware of the needs of those around me, or am I too self-focused to notice?
- Do I see how becoming a helpful, humble, thankful, hard working person gives me a better chance that people will be moved to help me if I'm in need?
- Do I ask the Lord to help the needy when He is asking me to help them?
- Am I careful, direct and shrewd in business?
- Do I think a healthy body guarantees conception, or do I realize God is the one Who enables conception?

Responses

- Father, thank you for blessing us, for sharing with us, for watching over us and meeting our needs.
- Thank you for being so kind to us.
- We are blessed to be your servant.

*"When someone
doesn't take responsibility
for their behavior
but just falls on their face
and puts everything on God,
that is called
Super Spiritual Passivity."*

the Authors

www.ingramcontent.com/pod-product-compliance
Lightning Source LLC
Chambersburg PA
CBHW020506030426
42337CB00011B/254